History of New Smyrna Black Businesses
With Present Area Businesses

Fannie Minson Hudson

ISBN 978-0-9792196-0-3
ISBN 0-9792196-0-4

Printed by
Copy Cat Printing Centers, Inc.
Edited by
Montez Nixon James
Published by
FANNIE MINSON HUDSON
699 West Street
New Smyrna Beach, FL 32168
Email: hnsbb@yahoo.com

Dedication

I dedicate this book to the Lord God who gave me life, and to my husband James E. Hudson, Sr., who is my life.

Trust in the LORD with all thine heart; and lean not unto thine own understanding. In all thy ways acknowledge him, and he shall direct thy paths. Amen. *(Proverbs 3:5-6)*

Acknowledgments

I want to recognize all of the Special People who gave unselfishly of their time, experiences, and personal information for this book; who willingly shared their lives in earnest holding nothing back, without them it would have been very difficult. I genuinely thank each of you from my heart. Fannie Minson Hudson.

A-B-C

Allen Chapel Mens' Day Committee

Jake Baker
Annie Mae Bell
Donald Bell
Lucy Bell
Mark Bell
Oretha Wyche Bell
Warrnon Bell, Sr.
Bethel Baptist Church, NSB
Black Heritage Museum
Ethel Davis Blake
Barbara Bobelak
Howard Boyd
LeFonia McDaniel Boyd
Debbie Marcisak Brendel
James Brendel
Alphonso Brown
Bernice Brown
Dorothy Lowery Brown
Pamela Brown
Vern Brown
Cathy Carlson, ARNP
Guy Clements
Mabel Catlin Carter
Vickie Cheeks
Annie Ruth Mullins Chisholm
Kelly Coates
Laura Coates
Neal Coates, Sr.
Neal Coates Jr.
Copy Cat Printing Centers, Inc.
Naomi Lee Cummings

D-E-F

Daytona Beach News-Journal
Dr. Lee Ann Davis
Sylvia Devaux
Tommie Devaux
Edgewater, City of, Leisure Services Department
Gail Davis Evans
Dr. Teresa Fagan, MD
Dr. James Flagg
Noeleen Skehan Foster
State Library and Archives of Florida
George Manuel Franklin
Jinnie Meeks Franklin

G-H-I

Gregory Gaskin
Billy (Bo) Graham
Mary Harrell
Derrick Harris
John Haygood
Rhonda Jordan Haynes
Dorothy Nance Hill
Eurcell (Jackie) Hives
Roosevelt Horne
James Hudson
Laura Hutchins

Patricia Plummer Gaskin
Felice Hankins
Darcia Warthaw Harris
Angie Hawkins
James (Choke) Haynes
Gail Henrikson
George Hill
Jimmy Lee Hives
Leroy (Buggy) Horne, Jr.
Hudson Plastering Se
Stacy Hutchins

J-K-L

Louella IsaacJackson
Celia Jones
Dwayne Jones
Viola Kallaham
R. Lynne Kunkle
Corzet Lawrence
Janice Lowry

Montez Nixon James
Darrell Jones
Jimmie Lee Kallaham
Rita Keen
Leroy Lane
Chad T. Lingenfelter
Gary Luther

M-N-O

Charles Mathis
Josie James Marshall
Charles McPhee
Cornelius Mitchell
John Montisano
Habibullah Mujahid
Pearl Henderson

Montez Nixon James
Darrell Jones
Jimmie Lee Kallaham
Rita Keen
Leroy Lane
Chad T. Lingenfelter
Gary Luther

New Smyrna Beach, City of
New Smyrna Beach Historic Preservation Commission
New Smyrna Museum of History

P-Q-R

Lynne Moore Plaskett
Freelove Cutter Pride
Ophelia Rainge
Christine Thomas Ricks
Veris (Mop Mop) Robinson
Gordon Rogers, Jr.
Zeb Russell

Russell Powell
Gwendolyn Rainge
Ralph Rainge
Dr. Nicole Robinson, MD
Arzy Rogers
Harold Lee Rouse

S-T-U

Peter Carl Shedrick
Garris Sherman
Edna Teemer
Claudette Thomas
R.C. (Robert) Thompson
Pete Tindle
Brenda Torres
UCF (University of Central Florida)
USF (University of South Florida)

Claude Shedrick
Lois Sims
Howard Teemer
Johnny Thomas
Pearlie Morris Thompson
Jack (J.T.) Tobler
Dr. Yong Tsai, MD

V-W-X

Volusia Magazine
Wanda Walker
Lavelle Waters
Antoinette White
Scott Whitfield
Rachel Wilcox
Arthur (Art) Williams
Anita James Wilson
Robert (Woody) Wilson
John Windon
Sandra Woodard
Willie A. Woods
Alexander Wynn, III

Helen Wadley
Jennifer Waters
Elizabeth (Liz) Whitaker
Calvin "Bear" White
T.C. Wilder
Sandy Winkler
Russelle Williams
Marjorie Williams Wilson
Theodore (Teddy) Wilson
Marie Walden Woodard
Harriet Woods
John Wooten

Y-Z

Katherine Wadley Zow

Sam Zow

TABLE OF CONTENTS

Introduction

It was a time when God and goodness was the law, and self-sufficiency was the order of the day. There was good and evil, right and wrong, and life was simpler. You could leave your doors wide open and everything remained in its place. All children in the neighborhood were treated equally, discipline and cookies for all. Living and loving was not taken for granted, everything was real and you understood where you stood at all times.

That time was the 1800 and 1900s and that place was the United States of America, that city was New Smyrna, Florida; those people were Blacks (Negro, Colored, or African Americans.)

One thing is for certain, these people were hard working and successful, because they used every available resource and opportunity for their advantage, and for the advancement and improvements of mankind. Do not get me wrong, there are people today with the same talents and reliability. However, it was different then because of so many new uncertainties and changes.

Every time I hear a story about those proud people of New Smyrna, my self-esteem and self worth grows and grows, and I want to tell the stories, no dressing-up or dressing-down, just the truth as it is being told.

At first glance, there is not much to see but just look again and the signs of the times are all there, waiting to come to life. You can feel the excitement, your heart begins to race, your breathing accelerates, you inhale a breath of fresh air, and suddenly you find what you were looking for, proud-ness and the realization that our fore parents did make a difference.

Take a drive through our neighborhoods and you will see all kinds of sights, run down buildings, empty lots, well kept homes, others homes not so well kept, both buildings and homes that might qualify as historical sites.

Even today, some homes and business could be restored, creating jobs and habitation for people of this community. With pride, hard work, adequate finances, guidance, and the understanding that we are all in this together, nothing is impossible for us to achieve. What affects one of us will affect us all.

The people of New Smyrna, Florida in the 1800s and 1900s had a lot to say and this is their song.

Let us go back in time and see what New Smyrna was like in the 1800s and 1900s west of the railroad tracks.

NOTE:
Because some dates could not be exact, approximate timelines are given. Also, a few addresses for businesses of the past have either changed or no longer exist today, for these addresses the street name may be used or street and block number if known.

TIMELINE

FLORIDA, VOLUSIA COUNTY, AND NEW SMYRNA FLORIDA

Until the year of Our Lord 1498, Florida was home to the Native American Indians.

1498 Florida was discovered and settled by people from Europe (Spanish and British.)

1768 Dr. Andrew Turnbull and others arrived here in New Smyrna Florida.

1775 Revolutionary War began.

1777 After the attempt to colonize New Smyrna failed Dr. Andrew Turnbull leaves.

1783 Revolutionary War ended.

1821 Florida became a territory of the United States of America.

1824 Mosquito County Florida formed.

1835 New Smyrna became the county seat for Mosquito County Florida.

1845 Florida became a state of the United States of America.

1850 Slave Schedule to the 1850 United State Census shows slave owners and number of slaves for Volusia County Florida.

3

1854	Volusia County Florida was formed from Orange County Florida.
1857 And 1859	The 1857 and 1859 Tax Roll of Volusia County Florida, showed slave owners and the number of slaves they had in their possessions for those years.
1860	Slave Schedule to the 1860 Census. Black and mulatto people bought, traded, or indentured servants were accounted for as slaves and considered the chattel (personal belongings) of their owners.
1861	Civil War of the United States began; the war was between the northern and southern states of the United States.
1862	Union Army organized the first Black troop units on the Georgia-Florida borders.
1863	President Abraham Lincoln is forever linked with freedom from slavery because of the Emancipation Proclamation he signed into effect in 1863. In addition to ending slavery, this meant freedom with very little or no financial and personal belonging, and no places to go. Without hope and determination this could have meant disaster.
1865	End of the Civil War (1861-1865) between the northern and southern states of the United States.

1870 The 1870 United State Census was the first ever census to record all race of people and especially the first overall grouping of the Black Race as Free people.

1885 Leroy Chisholm, a black man of Volusia County Florida registered 159+ acres of land with the United States Land Office.

1886 Mount Calvary Missionary Baptist Church (Black Church) of New Smyrna was organized.

1887 Blue Springs, Orange City and Atlantic Railroad (BSOCA) came to New Smyrna Florida.

1887 City of New Smyrna was incorporated.

1888 DeLand become county seat for Volusia County Florida.

1891 Allen Chapel African Methodist Episcopal Church (Black Church) of New Smyrna was organized.

1892 Florida East Coast Railroad (FEC) came to New Smyrna Florida. Many black people came to New Smyrna looking for work and prosperity.

1892 Saint Paul (Hickeynut) Methodist Episcopal Church (Black Church) of New Smyrna was organized.

1917-1918	World War I (WWI.)
1941-1945	World War II (WWII.)
1950-1953	Korean War.
1965-1973	Vietnam War.

Courtesy of SSW

2008 Map of the State of Florida

1832 Map of Mosquito County, Florida

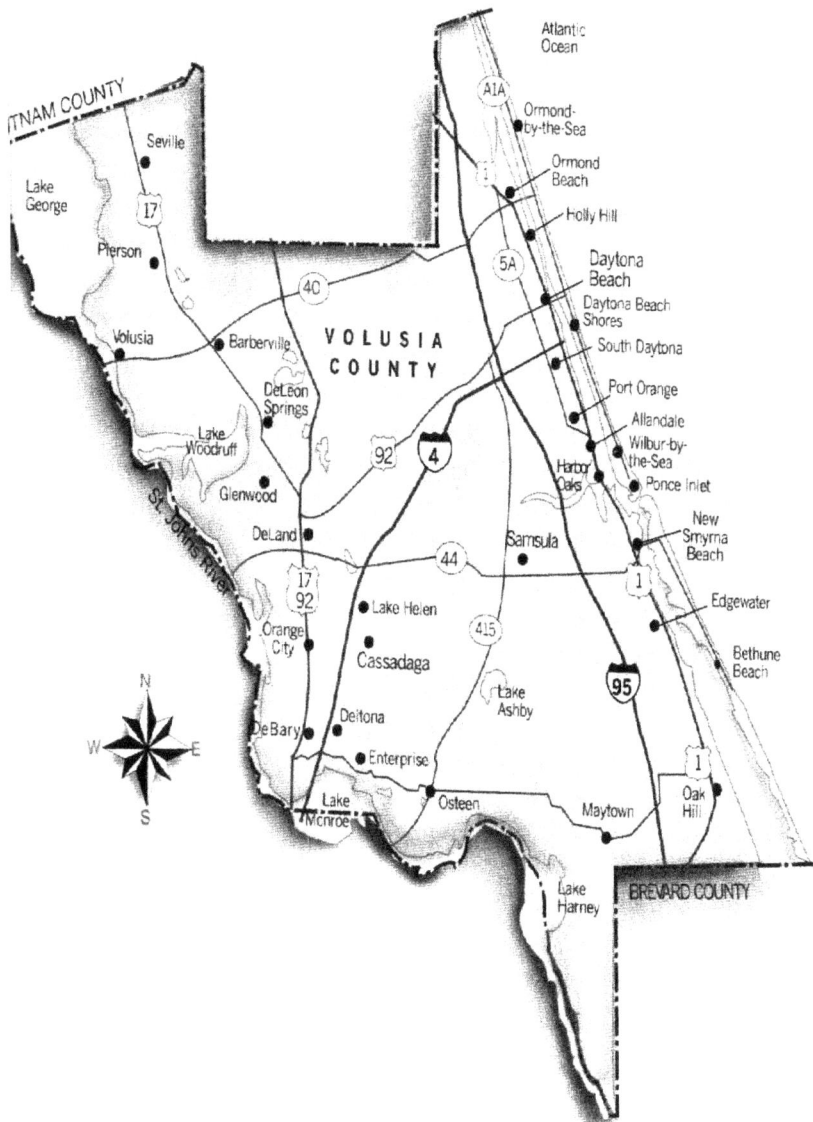

Courtesy of Volusia Magazine-Daytona Beach News-Journal

2006 Map of Volusia County Florida

9

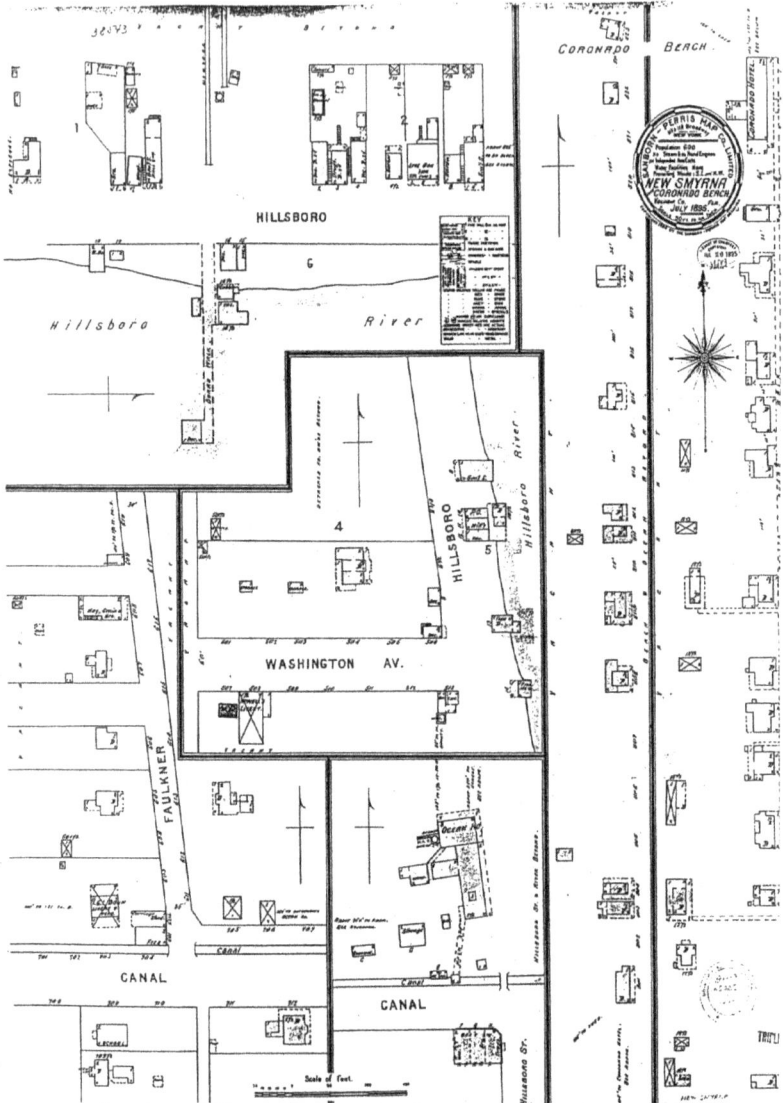

Courtesy of Historic Preservation Commission New Smyrna

1895 Sanborn Map of City of New Smyrna and Coronado Beach, Total population 600.

INDUSTRIES AND INCOME SOURCES

FOR NEW SMYRNA FLORIDA

FROM

THE LATE 1800s

TO ABOUT 1963

Courtesy of State Library and Archives of Florida

FISH, SHRIMP, AND CRAB INDUSTRIES

Courtesy of State Library and Archives of Florida

ORANGE GROVES
Volusia County Florida 1930

13

SAW MILL
E. W. Bonds Lumber Company
Lake Helen, Florida (1910)

Courtesy of Florida Library and Archives of Florida

FLORIDA EAST COAST RAILROAD

The Miamian, a train with a name, was surely a better working train. The Florida East Cost Railroad was the saving grace for many families in this town both black and white. Mr. Henry Flagler was a man with a heart and was known to be generous as well as kind to his workers. He helped them with housing, food, and hospital facilities. Mr. Flagler did these things for his workers at a time when the black community would not have been able to use the same medical facilities or any other facilities as whites. His intent was to treat all people as equals. The Florida East Coast Railroad came to New Smyrna Beach in the late 1890s and remained one of the biggest employers in this town until around 1963. Today some 100 years later you can see the trains and hear the horns blow as they come through the town. Mr. Flagler, we see and hear you loud and clear.[1]

----

[1]George Hill; Dorothy Hill: Louella Isaac Jackson; Warrnon Bell:Garris Sherman; Roosevelt Horne; Montez Nixon James

Courtesy of New Smyrna Museum of History

TURPENTINE INDUSTRIES

This turpentine still and turpentine mill was located in Samsula Florida, on the outskirts of New Smyrna. This establishment was in operation sometime in the 1920s and 30s, in other areas of Volusia County the Turpentine industry had already gone bust.

Working with turpentine is interesting work. The bark of the pine tree is scraped from the tree about waist high from the ground, a collection container is nailed to the tree where the bark was removed in the shape of a V so the sap from the tree would draw, and the raw gum from the pine tree fell in the container drop by drop. The gum dipper, a person that rode in a horse drawn wagon carrying large 100 gallon collection barrows, would stop and empty the collection contain from the pine tree into the barrow. Now, after a whole barrow of raw gum had been collected it was taken back to the turpentine mill and processed. The by products of the raw turpentine were, turpentine used for medicinal use, resin, and other useful products.[2]

---

[2]Warrnon Bell: Garris Sherman.

16

MANUAL LABOR

Black men working on flood-control ditches in New Smyrna in 1935. This work was considered by some to be blue collar jobs; by others these jobs were back breaking labor.

BUSINESSES

OF

THE

PAST

Washington Square
529-533 Washington Street

It is believed that sometime between 1920 and the early
1940s another building had occupied this same spot, and was
possibly owned by Leroy Chisholm. Other business that were
believed to have been housed here were the office a Dr.
McDaniel, and another business belonging to Rosa Lee
Banks, who supposedly rented rooms in the upstairs portion of
the old building. In 1945 Ellis (Sweet) and Willie Mae Meeks
Hill married and opened a restaurant, The Palace Café in the
new building Sweet Hill built from the foundation up by
himself. This building housed a restaurant and a dance hall,
and a pressing club (which was the name used in the 1900s
for dry cleaners.) For many years, other businesses occupied
space in the same units from time to time. In the 1940s and
50s this building was similar to the present day strip mall,
where a group of stores provided different services or
products. Today the west unit is the location of George
Manuel Franklin's business, the OK Barber Shop. [3]

---

[3]Willie Mae Hill; Louella Isaac; George Hill; Dorothy Hill; Johnny Thomas;
Marie Walden Woodard; George Manuel Franklin; Roosevelt Horne;
Montez Nixon James.

Louise Rogers Beauty Shop
522 Washington Street
New Smyrna Beach, FL

In 1950, Louise Rogers beauty shop was where many newly trained beauticians learned their trade. In 1957 the beauty shop was on the first floor of a two story building situated next door to the So-So Playhouse Restaurant on the east and the Wallace Building on the west. Mrs. Rogers may have been sister to Elizabeth Colley.[4]

Wallace Building
524 Washington Street
New Smyrna Beach, FL

James and Clara Wallace owned the Wallace Building, it had two stories and was located across the street from Saint Paul A.M.E. Church. The Wallace's lived upstairs and rented the two areas downstairs. They also owned a garage apartment building two door over from their house, on the southeast corner of Washington and Dimmick Street. It was stated that John Watson owner of the Watson Building at 530 Washington Street in 1930s was the brother of Clara Wallace.[5]

Watson Building
530 Washington Street
New Smyrna Beach, FL

John and Mina Watson were owners of a store at this address in the 1930s. The store was a favorite place for children to stop for ice cream and sodas after Church. Reportedly John was the brother of Clara Wallace the owner of another two story building at 524 Washington Street at that time.[6]

---

[4]Johnny Thomas; Marie Walden Woodard; Willie Mae Meeks Hill.
[5]Johnny Thomas; United States Census 1930.
[6]United States Census 1930.

20

Barber Shop
539 Washington
New Smyrna Beach, FL

Before becoming a barbershop in the 1940s this building was the restaurant of Mrs. Lydia Pettis, past community humanitarian. Afterward, it was the restaurant of Mary Prescott's mother.

Then in the 1950s it was the barbershop of Will Meeks.

Next it was the barbershop of Willie Reese who was also called "Barber" Reese."[7]

---

[7]George Manuel Franklin; Garris Sherman; Johnny Thomas.

21

Mary Prescott Beauty Shop
541 Washington
New Smyrna Beach, FL

In the 1940s Mary Prescott was a self-employed beautician with a home based business. The beauty shop was on the front porch part of the resident, and the balance of the house was the living quarters. [8]

---

[8]Marie Walden Woodard; Louella Isaac Jackson; Johnny Thomas.

Catherine Ratcliff
553 Washington Street
New Smyrna Beach, FL

In the 1930s and 1940s Catherine's beauty shop was next door to Mt. Calvary Baptist Church. It was also the beauty shop of Vicki Wadley around the late 1980s and early 1990s.[9]

Big Cliff's
578 Washington Street
New Smyrna Beach, FL

Clifford "Big Cliff" Williams, father of Michael Williams, owned and operated a restaurant, juke joint and an apartment unit. The restaurant and juke joint were downstairs on the first floor, and the apartment was on the second floor. At Big Cliff's in the 1940s and 50s a customer could get a full meal for 25 cents. For example a chicken dinner came with two side orders of vegetables, a dessert, and a drink. The menu carried such specialties as hog chitlings (pig innards cooked to a perfection), stew beef, pork chops, liver and onions, etc.[10]

---

[9]George Hill: Johnny Thomas; George Manuel Franklin.
[10]George Hill; Dorothy Hill; Montez Nixon James.

23

Smyrna Funeral Home
570 Washington Street
New Smyrna Beach, FL

From the 1940s until the 1960s Mildred Smith managed Smyrna Funeral Home in the black community, for a white man by the name of Willis Settle.[11]

Then sometime in the 1970s this same building was the site for a funeral business owned by Dr. Rabie Gainous.

Today it is the location of Gainous-Wynn Funeral Home owned by Alexander Wynn III.

---

[11]T. C. Wilder: Johnny Thomas; James Hudson, Sr.; George Hill.

Catlin Grocery Store/Masonic Lodge
582 Washington Street
New Smyrna Beach, FL

The Catlin's moved to New Smyrna from Volco during the depression in 1928. During that time the sawmill industry in Volco went bust.

Norman and Ollie Catlin owned and operated a grocery store on the first floor of the Masonic Hall at 582 Washington Street.

The store was in operation from 1931 to around the late 60s or early 70s. Norman purchased the grocery store from a white man by the name of Gilbolt. Mr. Gilbolt's former store was located at 409 Mary Avenue, where Karen's Restaurant was until recently, and where JC's Restaurant is located today.

When Norman first purchased the grocery store from Mr. Gilbolt, he moved it to its first location on Sheldon Street, and from there it was moved to the final location at the Masonic Hall on Washington Street, which was at that time located next door to the old Chisholm High School. The store sold groceries, ice cream, meats, fruits, vegetables, as well as cookies and candies.[12]

---

[12]Mable Catlin Carter; Dorothy Nance Hill; George Hill; Johnny Thomas; James Hudson, Sr.; Sandra Woodard; Rhonda Jordon Haynes; Montez Nixon James.

Oscar and Virginia Anderson
596 Washington Street
New Smyrna Beach, FL

From the 1930s through the mid 1950s the Anderson's owned a café, a store, and a rooming house. The store and café were located at 596 Washington Street, which is now the parking lot at the northwest corner of the Alonzo "Babe" James Community Center. Their rooming house was located on the southeast corner of Myrtle Avenue and Washington Street. In addition to regular food on the menu, mullet fish sandwiches and pigs feet could be bought for only 10 cents each.

When Virginia became ill and was no longer able to tend the store Oscar and Pearl Lemon Anderson, her son and daughter-in-law assumed operation and management of the store and café. Regular food items were not the only fare on the menu, hot dogs and snow cones were a favorite treat for children of all ages. Pearl Anderson was the aunt of Robert (R.C.) and Pearlie Mae Morris Thompson, who are the son-in-law and daughter of Burkey and Pearl Henderson Williams Morris, and the grandson-in-law and granddaughter of Henry and Hattie Henderson.[13]

---

[13]Robert (R.C.) Thompson; Pearlie Morris Thompson; United States Census 1930.

Harry and Lillie Walker
585 Washington
New Smyrna Beach, FL

Nursing Home/Hospital/Hand Laundry, Café, Meat Market, and Rooming House

According to the 1930 Census of the United States, Pompie "Harry" and Lillie Walker operated a rooming house in their home. Years later, they owned and operated several businesses. They were reported to have had a café, a meat market, a hand laundry, a nursing home, and a hospital. At the hand laundry all washing and ironing of clothing were done by the hands of the hired help.

The hospital located on the northeast corner of Myrtle Avenue and Washington Street was reported to be a birthing hospital for black women, it had a blue rooms for boys and pink rooms for girls.

The nursing home located directly behind the hospital provided care for the elderly from the community and surrounding towns for long or short term stays. The hospital and nursing home were still in operation in the late 1960. Harry worked for Florida East Coast Railroad and help Lillie with the businesses they owned.

It was stated that Lillie had another hospital at one time located directly across the street from her house on the northeast corner of Sheldon and Washington Street. It is believed that Lillie herself was a nurse, she always wore white and demanded that her help wear white while caring for the sick in her care. Lillie was a no nonsense person and demanded perfection from others. She was a humanitarian in her own right, and a voice for the black people of New Smyrna in the 1950s and later.[14]

---

[14]Freelove Cutter Pride; Rosemary Moore; Louella Isaac Jackson; Mable Catlin Carter; Zeb Russell; Dorothy Hill; Marie Walden Woodard; United States Census 1930.

Parker and Mizell Meeks
440 North Myrtle Avenue
New Smyrna Beach, FL

Parker and Mizell were second generation post-slavery business owners. They owned a grocery store in the late 1920s to around 1954. Mizell managed the store located on the same property as their house, and Parker worked as an oiler on the railroad. The house and the store no longer exist today, but their contributions to this community live on.[15]

---

[15]Marie Walden Woodard; R. Lynne Kunkle; United States Census 1930; Gail Davis Evans

William "Cat" Hunter
462 Myrtle Avenue
New Smyrna Beach, FL

William "Cat" Hunter, grandfather of Darryl Fullington, retired NFL (National Football League) Free Safety, in the 1950s was a self employed ice vendr. In the 1940s and earlier Ice in large 25-50 pound blocks were used in the home ice box to keep foods fresh, and in stores and restaurants to keep food, produce, and drinks cold.[16]

---

[16]Garris Sherman; Dorothy Nance Hill; Christine Thomas Ricks; Felice Hankins; Montez Nixon James; Rhonda Jordan Haynes.

Lowery Rooming House
436 Myrtle and Enterprise
New Smyrna Beach, FL

In 1920 John and Anna Stubbs, owned this building, the first floor was used as their living quarters, and rooms were rented on the second floor. Next the Redemptive Fathers from the Catholic Church brought this building, and it became the Madonna House. Nuns (also called Sisters) managed it as a Community Center. In the 1950s while working at the Madonna House, Annie Lowery learned that the building was going to be vacated by the Church. She inquired about it, and was given the first opportunity to purchase it. Her family moved in on the first floor, and rented out rooms on the second floor to men from surrounding towns working with the railroad. There were six rooms on the second floor and a kitchen available for use by roomers to prepare their own meals. In 1986 the building was marked for demolishing, and their daughter, Dorothy Lowery Brown assumed management of it, rehabilitated it, and converted it to duplex apartments. That same years J.W. and Annie moved to their new home, built for them by their daughter next door to her own home.[17]

---

[17]Dorothy Lowery Brown; Volusia County Property Tax Roll, 1925-30.

31

Clareese Everett Beauty Shop
North Duss Street
New Smyrna Beach, FL

Clareese Everett beauty shop was located at the back of her home. She was from the old school of beauticians that specialized in pressing and curling hair only and did not believe in using chemicals on the hair. She was still performing beauty services in the early 1980.[18]

---

[18]Fannie Minson Hudson; Montez Nixon James.

Howard Loveless
Duss Street
New Smyrna Beach, FL

In the 1950s, 60s and 70s Howard Loveless, self made enterpriser and self-employed handyman, father figure, and mentor to many youths in the community would drive around town looking for an opportunity to create a job for youths wanting to better themselves. He used every available resource at his disposal to teach and share his talents. He was an inspiration, motivator and mentor for many youths in this community.[19]

Coates Auto-Body Repair Shop
1501 Enterprise Avenue
New Smyrna Beach, FL

Neal (Big Neal) and Laura Coates, were owners of an auto body shop business from 1978 to 1985, located first at 1501 Enterprise Avenue in New Smyrna Beach, and later moved to Ridgewood Avenue in Edgewater, FL. In addition to operating the shop, Neal worked full-time at Daytona Beach Community College as an instructor. Today, Neal is a minister of the Gospel and spends his free time doing volunteer work in the community. Neal and wife Laura reside in New Smyrna Beach, FL. [20]

---

[19]Donald Bell; Warrnon Bell; Oretha Wyche Bell; Montez Nixon James.
[20]Neal (Big Neal) Coates; Laura Coates; Fannie Minson Hudson.

Mary Jackson
605 Duss Street
New Smyrna Beach, FL

Mary Jackson's Beauty Shop was on the south side of her home. She was in business around the early 60s until the 1980s. Hair chemical were not used at this establishment the straightening comb and curling iron were the tools of the trade.[21]

---

[21]Harold Lee Rouse; Gail Davis Evans; Marjorie Williams Wilson.

Johnny and Mattie Waters
1201 Enterprise Avenue
New Smyrna Beach, FL

Johnny and Mattie Waters, great-grandparents of Wes Chandler retired NFL *(National Football League)* Wide Receiver, and great-great-grandparents of Dallas Baker, Jr., University of Florida Wide Receiver, had a home based taxicab business from 1954 through 1975. In addition to owning the taxicab business Johnny worked full-time in the railway yards with Florida East Coast Railroad for 40 plus years.[22]

---

[22]Christine Thomas Ricks; Felice Hankins; Montez Nixon James.

478 Palm Street
New Smyrna Beach, FL

This building located on the southeast corner of Ronnoc Lane and Palm Street was originally the rooming house and home to the family of Dewey and Willie Clark, later it was owned by Herman Frazier. And in the 1960s this building was purchased by Daisy Davis as a family home for the Davis Family.

Today it is the private residence of the granddaughter of Daisy Davis. [23]

---

[23]Gail Davis Evans.

Pete Freeman
Palm Street
New Smyrna Beach, FL

In the early 1930s to the late 1950s Pete Freeman pioneer investor, realtor, landlord and part owner of a funeral home in Daytona Beach was known as one of New Smyrna's leading landlord-homeowner. [24]

Davis Grocery Store
558 Ronnoc Lane
New Smyrna Beach, FL

The grocery store and later the convenience store was owned by Clinton and Daisy Davis, it was conveniently located across the street from the New Chisholm High School on Ronnoc Lane (which is Chisholm Elementary School today), sometimes the children would go over and spend their lunch money for snacks. At one time, the Davis Grocery Store also had a bakery, sold meats, and groceries, later years it sold miscellaneous items including cookies and candies and can goods. This business was in operation from the 1930s to some time after 1970. [25]

---

[24]Montez Nixon James.
[25]Gail Davis Evans: Jimmie Hives; Johnny Thomas; Sylvia Deuvax; Garris Sherman.

Colley Grocery Store
549 Charlovix
New Smyrna Beach, FL

Colley Grocery Store was owned and operated by Elizabeth Colley. This store provided service to the community until the early 1970s. Elizabeth sold dry good, cookies, sodas, kerosene fuel for cooking and oil for lamp-lights. Elizabeth was the mother of Idell Davis, the grandmother of Myrna Freeman wife of actor Morgan Freeman, and sister of Louise Rogers, owner of Rogers Beauty Shop. [26]

Blue Goose Restaurant
Floyd's Grocery Store and Juke Joint
566 Charlovix
New Smyrna Beach, FL

This location at one time served as grocery store, a restaurant and a juke joint from the late 1940s to about 1970. Frank Floyd and daughter Bee were proprietors of this establishment. It was a late night to early morning kind of place. An individual could hangout in the juke joint all night and go directly to work from there, because breakfast could be purchased at the restaurant the next morning. The grocery store would permit members of the community to get groceries and food items on credit and allow them to pay for it on payday or Friday when they got their checks. [27]

---

[26]Johnny Thomas; Garris Sherman: Polk City Directory 1950-1970.
[27]Howard Boyd, Jimmie Lee Kallaham, Sylvia Devaux.

Boss Man's Place
Hickory Street
New Smyrna Beach, FL

Today this building is an apartment complex, located on the northeast corner of Hickory Street and Mary Avenue. It was a teenage gathering place, a store and a resident for the owner and operator Mr. Harris (Boss Man.) As a teenager in the 1960s, Boss Man's was the place to be seen. Boss Man lived up stairs on the second floor of the building; the downstairs portion or first floor contained two separate businesses, one part was the grocery and convenience store, sold cookies and candies; and the other part of the building teenagers meet and danced to music from the jukebox. [28]

---

[28]George Hill; Dorothy Nance Hill; Jack (JT) Tobler; Leroy (Buggy) Horne, Jr.; Christine Ricks: Felice Hankins; Charles McPhee; James (Choke) Haynes; Rhonda Jordan Haynes.

JY Jackson Bar-B-Que Restaurant
303 Hickory Street
New Smyrna Beach, FL

JY (James) and Louella Isaac Jackson own this historical business establishment. It was an all night gathering spot for the public on the weekend from the 1940s until 1989, during that time the Jackson's sold soul food, beer, and wine. This local restaurant may have been one of the first privately owned integrated eating establishment in the city, where people of all races and social economic backgrounds would purchase food sit and eat it on the spot, then order more food to take home. Upon request Mr. and Mrs. Jackson, would ship bar-b-que meats overnight by airplane all over Florida, Georgia, and Mississippi. Today the restaurant is no longer open to the public, but bar-b-que meats are still prepared for special affairs. [29]

---

[29]Louella Isaac Jackson; George Hill; Dorothy Nance Hill; James Hudson; Fannie Hudson.

40

Lowery Service Station and Garage
1501 Enterprise Avenue
New Smyrna Beach, FL

The Lowery Service Station and Garage was built in 1952 by John (J. W.) and Annie Lowery. It was a full service gas station and had a two bay garage, with a dedicated mechanic named J. W. Lowery. Years before this business was established, J. W. had a dream to one day be the owner of a service station and garage. In the 1950s J.W. worked full-time for Florida East Coast Railroad, and on his off time worked as a mechanic at 515 Mary Avenue, where he rented garage space from Mrs. Inez Brooks.

An avid fan of television J. W. never missed the news of the day. One night in the 1950s he was watching television, a millionaire by the name of Mr. Hughes, living in Daytona Beach at that time, was on the news, at that very moment, this man gave J.W. the hope and inspiration needed to make the dream of owning a service station a reality.

That night J.W. told his wife Annie and daughter Dorothy, he was going to see Mr. Hughes the next morning. Sure enough, the next morning J.W. went to see Mr. Hughes, to sell his dream and to ask for help with the service station.

41

They met and talked, Mr. Hughes did not loan J.W. the money, but called the bank and vouched for him promising to pay the money back to the bank if J.W. was not able to do it himself.

From 1978 to 1985, Neal (Big Neal) and Laura Coates owned and operated an auto-body shop at this address.

Today, Airport Auto Air & Service owned and operated by Guy Clements and John Wooten occupies this building.[30]

---

[30]Neal (Big) Coates; Laura Coates; Guy Clements; John Wooten; Dorothy Lowery Brown.

Fred and Cora Meeks Alderman Boarding House
440 Julia Street
New Smyrna Beach, FL

According to Volusia County property appraisers records this building was built around 1903. In 1930, this was the home and rooming house of a Masouri Bohler. Next, Fred and Cora Meeks Alderman owned and operated a boarding house at this address in the 1940s. At that time most of the guests were firemen and other men working on the railroad, who usually lived here during the week and went home to their families on days off and the weekends. There were eight guest rooms on the second floor, the Alderman family lived on the first floor; the boarding house also prepared and served meals for their guests. The building is no longer used as a boarding house. Today it is the family home of Charles and Marvalyn Mathis, grandson-in-law and granddaughter of Fred and Cora Meeks Alderman.[31]

---

[31]Charles Mathis; Marvalyn Mathis; Johnny Thomas; Roosevelt Horne; James Hudson; George Hill; Fredia Crosby Mitchell.

Courtesy of Black Heritage Museum

Moon Bar
503 Julia Street
New Smyrna Beach, FL

In the 1930s this building housed a dry cleaner and tailor shop owned by Oscar Meeks. Sometime after that, it became a liquor store and was owned by a white man and managed by a black man named Clemy Brown.

Later it was purchased by Harold Marshall and became the first African American owned bar west of the railroad tracks. The original liquor license used to sell liquor is reported to have been purchased from a local casino establishment. Besides being the first black owned bar it was also the smallest, if seven people including the bartender were inside all at one time, it was crowded leaving very little wiggle room.

From 1956-1972, Harold and wife Josie also owned Deon's Restaurant a building next door at 509½ Julia and later at 524 Julia. At Deon's you could purchase sandwiches and sodas, this building also had a patio out back where children met to socialize.[32]

---

[32]Josie James Marshall; United States Census 1930; George Hill; Johnny Thomas; Roosevelt Horne.

Nellie Alderman Marshall's Grocery Store
509 Julia Street
New Smyrna Beach, FL

Preston and Nellie Alderman Marshall were proprietors of a café During the same time period (April 1930) this address, 511 Julia Street was the residents of a David Burley Family. Sometime after that, this location became the grocery store of Preston and Nellie, selling homemade cakes and pies, and groceries. In addition to the store, they had a rooming house located directly behind the store, as well as three other houses located directly behind that rooming house. Deon's Restaurant located next door on the east side of the grocery store, at 509 Julia was operated by Harold and Josie Marshall, son and daughter-in-law of Preston and Nellie, in the 1950s.[33]

[33]George Hill; Louella Isaac Jackson; Johnny Thomas; Roosevelt Horne.

45

The Skin House
514 Julia Street
New Smyrna Beach, FL

The Skin House a local gambling establishment where bets were wagered, monies won and lost, was first located on Julia Street somewhere between 527-551 Julia. As the stories goes, when the old rundown building was demolished the gaming establishment was relocated across the street to 514 Julia Street. Its been said the reason gambling establishments were called skin houses was, the owner of the house always got a portion of all winnings before the winner got to take the money, thus called cutting off the top. The second reason was most gamblers usually left broke; their pockets were skinned or clean out because the house had eventually gotten all of their money. In the end, this skin house too was in bad condition and was demolished as well. In the background on the left is the Thompson's Rooming at 124 Railroad Street.[34]

---

[34]George Hill; Johnny Thomas; Roosevelt Horne; James (Choke) Haynes: R. Lynne Kunkle.

46

Courtesy of City of New Smyrna

Clarence and Rosetta Chappell Cafe
515 Julia Street
New Smyrna Beach, FL

In April 1930, Mary Powell and her mother Callie Beasley operated a café at this location 515 Julia Street. Years later, from the early 1950s through the mid 1970s Clarence and Rosetta Chappell owned and operated a café and juke joint here. Their café sold sandwiches, beer and wine, and had an area for dancing. The building is no longer standing it was demolished.[35]

---

[35]George Hill; Johnny Thomas; Roosevelt Horne; Polk's City Directory 1950-1975.

The Central Bar
519 Julia Street
New Smyrna Beach, FL

In the 1930s, 519 Julia Street was the homestead of Jackson and Cora Buck. In the early 1950s Roosevelt Horne purchased this building from the Buck's and converted it into a rooming house for men working on new road construction for US1 (Dixie Freeway.) In the late 1960s George and Louise Butler brought this property from Roosevelt Horne and had him to build the Central Bar. In addition to owning and operating this bar, the Butler's owned a restaurant and poolroom in Daytona Beach on the old Second Avenue (Dr. Mary McLeod Bethune Boulevard.) The alcoholic beverage license used for selling beer, liquor, and wine was reported to have been purchased from another business establishment closing at the southeast corner of Julia Street and Orange Avenue, where Jessup's Pawn Shop is located today. The Central Bar building has been owned and operated by several people since the Butler's. In 1999, Freddie Mann purchased the building and converted it to a poolroom called the Honey Room.[36]

---

[36]George Hill; Johnny Thomas; George Manuel Franklin; Roosevelt Horne.

48

524 Julia Street
New Smyrna Beach, FL

This building originally had two stories, the upstairs was used as a rooming house and the downstairs portion was a restaurant.

In 1930 a café owned and operated by Charlotte Holzendorft was at this address.

Sometime after 1930 the two story building was converted to a single floor building.

In the 1940s and early 50s Nancy Richards aunt of Josie Marshall owned and operated a restaurant in one half of the building and lived in the other half.

Afterward Leroy and Ola Mae Lipsey managed a restaurant here also.

Next, Roosevelt Horne operated a Tavern and Restaurant here

Finally, Josie and husband Harold owned and operated Deon's Restaurant and Sandwich Shop across the street at 509½ Julia, and later at this address 524 Julia until 1972.

Today this building serves as a private resident.[37]

---

[37]George Hill; Johnny Thomas; Roosevelt Horne; Fifteenth Census of the United: 1930; Josie Marshall.

Green Leaf Restaurant
Leroy Bass Juke Joint and Cafe
527 Julia Street
New Smyrna Beach, FL

Elijah Campbell was the owner of a cafe in this location around 1930-1945; located on the northwest corner of Julia and Dimmick Streets.

In the 1950s this location was owned and operated by Myrtis Davis Smith. It had a juke joint and sold snacks, beer and wine.

Some years later in the mid 1950 in the same location, a juke joint was owned and operated by Leroy Bass.

In the early 1980s, Louis (Hambone) Love and Gwendolyn Rainge owned this juke joint in addition to another juke joint in Oak Hill, Florida, in an area of town called Shiloh.

The old building at this location has been gone for many years, today this location is part of housing belonging to the Central Florida Community Development Corporation.[38]

---

[38]George Hill; Dorothy Nance Hill; Johnny Thomas; Gwendolyn Rainge; Roosevelt Horne.

The Star Theater
535 Julia Street
New Smyrna Beach, FL

In the 1940, and 50s the black community boasted its own movie theater. It was operated by a white man. The best part of having this theatre in the neighborhood during segregation was black people could sit anywhere they wanted during the movies and not be afraid.[39]

Jessie's Playhouse
529 and 550 Julia Street
New Smyrna Beach, FL

In the 1930s and 1940s Ms. Jessie Aycot, owned and operated a juke joint, sold beer, wine, snacks and sandwiches; and provide a space for dancing as well. Jessie later sold this business to Leroy Bass, and started another business at 550 Julia Street. It was located on the southeast corner of Julia and Lewis Street. This same building and business was owned and operated by Roosevelt and Lee Woulard Horne for many years, and ceased to operate sometime around 1990.

Today a new building is under construction to house the New Smyrna Beach branch of the National Church of God.[40]

---

[39]George Hill; Gwendolyn Rainge; Johnny Thomas; Roosevelt Horne; Polk's City Directory 1950.
[40]George Hill; Johnny Thomas; Roosevelt Horne.

Roosevelt's Playhouse
541 Julia Street
New Smyrna Beach, FL

Roosevelt Horne owned his first business, a restaurant in 1947, located at 219 Dimmick Street. From there the restaurant moved to 524 Julia Street, and became a Tavern and Restaurant. Not one to settle for less than his best, Roosevelt attended Bethune-Cookman College and in 1949 graduated with credentials to become a General Building Contractor.

In the early 1950s he moved the tavern and restaurant from 524 Julia Street to 550 Julia Street, (the southeast corner of Julia and Lewis Street), which had been the business of Jessie Aycott. In addition to being a building contractors and operating the tavern and restaurant Roosevelt also owned a rooming house at 519 Julia Street from 1950 to the late 1960s. He later sold that property to George and Louise Butler, and built the Central Bar to their specifications.

In 1964 Roosevelt and wife Lee moved the tavern and restaurant for the last and final time to 541 Julia Street, and it became Roosevelt's Playhouse a night club and eating place, and was in operation until their retirement in 1990.

From the beginning of his career as building contractor until his retirement Roosevelt was responsible for numerous houses and buildings being erected, remodeled and rehabilitated in the community. As a concerned citizen Roosevelt volunteered for public service by attending meeting and sitting on City Boards to represent people of the community. Around 2003 the property at 541 Julia Street was sold, and the new owners demolished the old building.

Today a new building is under construction to house the New Smyrna Beach branch of the National Church of God. Roosevelt's wife Lee Woulard Horne was the niece of Ola Mae Robinson, the owner of a juke joint at 343 Palms Street.[41]

---

[41]Roosevelt Horne; George Hill; Johnny Thomas; James Hudson, Sr.

Nina Stanley Rooming House and Restaurant
551 Julia Street
New Smyrna Beach, FL

Built around 1926 this building was the home, rooming house, and restaurant of Jasper and Nina Stanley. Meals consisted of several courses and were served for breakfast, lunch, and dinner 7 days a week. Anyone in the community and out of town visitors could stop by for food sit and eat or take it home. Customers were always there for food because it was plentiful and it was an all you could eat buffet style food service. One gentleman who went regularly (on a daily basis) said "in fact Ms. Nina served the best food in town during the 1940s and 1950s." It is believed that Nina and Virginia Jones the owner of a rooming house at 336 Palm Street were sisters.[42]

---

[42]George Hill; Johnny Thomas; Ophelia Rainge; Fredia Crosby Mitchell.

Clark Used Car Sales
554-58 Julia Street
New Smyrna Beach, FL

In the 1950s Ellis and Luscious Clark owned a used car lot and mechanic shop at the southwest corner of Julia and Lewis Street. In the 1960s this same business was the Clark Diner, the Clark Paradise Inn and Clark's Motel. The diner was reported to have a ice cream parlor inside where the young folks would meet. Today that site is the parking lot for the Volusia County Health Department. This same business was at one time a self service launderette.[43]

Rogers and Robinson Shoe Repair Shop
Railroad Street
New Smyrna Beach, FL

Gordon Rogers, Sr., owned a shoe repair shop in the late 1940s and early 1950s, on Railroad Street directly behind the Spot Restaurant and Tourist Home. Later in 1954 this same shoe repair shop was operated by Dan and Thelma Robinson. [44]

Liza Lewis Kindergarten
Palm Street
New Smyrna Beach, FL

Liza, mother of Curtis Wooten, operated a private kindergarten in her home at this address on Palm Street for many years.[45]

---

[43] Johnny Thomas; George Hill; Roosevelt Horne; Polk City Directory 1960.
[44] Johnny Thomas; Roosevelt Horne; Arzy Rogers; Gordon Rogers, Jr
[45] Dorothy Nance Hill; Marie Walden Woodard.

Courtesy of City of New Smyrna Beach

David and Cora Thompson Rooming House
124 Railroad Street
New Smyrna Beach, FL

This neighborhood was called Reno. From the look of the outside window shutters this rooming house was quite grand in size and beauty during its heydays in the 1930s, 1940s, and 1950s. The Thompson family lived on one floor and rented rooms on the other. This building is no longer standing it was demolished.[46]

---

[46]Louella Isaac Jackson; George Hill; Johnny Thomas; Roosevelt Horne, R. Lynne Kunkle; Garris Sherman.

Snooks Place
Star-Lite Beer Garden
225 Dimmick Street
New Smyrna Beach, FL

This business was first owned by Henry and Rosa Smith. Sometimes during the 1930s and 40s Rudolph and Estella Thompson brought this business from the Smith, and they cooked and sold bar-b-que. Next in the mid 1940s Willie (Snooks) and Naomi Lee Cumming purchased the business from Rudolph and Estella Thompson. Snook's juke joint sold beer, wine, sodas, and snacks. Snooks Place was also known as the Star-Lite Beer Garden.

In addition to being a restaurant this business served as the dispatch station for cab or taxi services during the 1950s. Snooks operate this business for approximately 50 years until his health began to fail in the 1990s.

From the 1990s until 2006, this same building housed Al's Sports Bar owned and operated by Al and Phalease Hill, son-in-law and daughter of Willie (Snook) and Naomi Cummings.

The original north half of this building was joined to the south half in the 1990s, which had in years past housed the store and juke joint of Higgs and Son.[47]

---

[47]Naomi Lee Cummings; George and Dorothy Nance Hill; Johnny Thomas; Roosevelt Horne' Montez Nixon James.

Higgs and Son
223 Dimmick
New Smyrna Beach, FL

In the 1940s this store and juke joint was owned and operated by Richard Higgs, the father of Robert Higgs. In the mid 1950s it became known as Higgs and Son, until Richard's illness forced him to retire. After Richard's retirement Robert operated this business until the mid 1960s. The store sold chips, candy, sodas, beer, wine, pigs feet, cigarettes, and peanuts. Higgs was located next door to Snooks' Place. Today both buildings (Snooks' Place and Robert Higgs Store and Juke Joint) are joined together making it one building, and served as Al's Sports Bar until mid 2006.[48]

---

[48]Johnny Thomas; Roosevelt Horne; Naomi Lee Cummings; Dorothy Nance Hill.

Eugene Thomas Pool Hall
219 Dimmick Street
New Smyrna Beach, FL

As a young man in the 1930s Eugene worked in a pool hall as the manager in addition to working another job downtown as a shoe shine boy or boot black. Later on Eugene and Annie Thomas, parents of Minister Johnny Thomas, purchased this same pool hall from the Smiths. The building had two sections one used by Eugene for a pool hall, the other section of the building was shared with Arsenior and her husband Tony the owners of The Spot. Eugene and Annie were operators of a restaurant in the 1940s on the now vacant lot on the west side of 518 Washington Street. [49]

The Spot
219 Dimmick Street
New Smyrna Beach, FL

Charles "Tony" and Arsenior McClendon, operated the Spot Restaurant, they sold dinners, platters, drinks, fast prepared food items (hot dogs, hamburgers) as well as having a place for dancing. The Spot was a very classy place. In 1950s Virginia McClendon Nance sister of Charles "Tony" operated the business.[50]

---

[49] Johnny Thomas; Roosevelt Horne; George Manuel Franklin.
[50] Johnny Thomas; Dorothy Nance Hill: Roosevelt Horne; George Manuel Franklin.

61

Davis and Franklin Barbershop
215 Dimmick Street
New Smyrna Beach, FL

In 1948 Arthur Davis and George Manuel Franklin owned and operated a barbershop next door to Eugene Thomas Pool Hall. It was part of an L shape building owned by the Smith's and was on the first floor level adjoined to a two story building. Arthur Davis was the son-in-law of Eugene Thomas. George Manuel Franklin continues to provide barber services today at 529-533 Washington Street in the building west unit. [51]

Rufus Wadley Beauty Shop
Beach Street
Daytona Beach, FL

Rufus (Uncle Rufus) lived in New Smyrna Beach, however he and wife Helen owned and operated a multi-station beauty shop in Daytona Beach on Beach Street next door to the United States Post Office. The shop was in operation in the 1980s and 1990s. Uncle Rufus was very patient and could be counted on to provide hair care on short notice, (wedding, proms, anniversaries, etc.) He was also a master cake baker readily sharing delicious treats with his customers.[52]

---

[51]George Manuel Franklin; Rhonda Jordan Haynes.
[52]Fannie Minson Hudson; Annie Ruth Mullins Chisholm.

Courtesy of Rhonda Jordan Haynes

Spot Café and Tourist Home
Society's Place
219 Dimmick
New Smyrna Beach, FL

Henry and Rosa Lee Smith owned a building made in an L shape having a one and two story portion. The one story portion was the barbershop of Arthur Davis and George Manuel Franklin. The two story portion of the same building had rooms for rent upstairs, and on the first floor there was a juke joint, where food, beer and wine were sold. In the mid 1960s Leandrus Jordan operated the northern portion of this building known as Society's Place.[53]

---

[53]Johnny Thomas; Roosevelt Horne; George Manuel Franklin;James (Choke) Haynes; Rhonda Jordan Haynes.

The Jones and Jordan Rooming House
336 Palm Street
New Smyrna Beach, FL

This long-ago structure was built sometime before the 1930s and served as a family home as well as a rooming house. The original owners James and Virginia Jones built this two story building upon the advice of a confidant who suggested they rent rooms to men working on the railroad.

It is believed that Virginia and Nina Stanley the owner of a rooming house at 551 Julia Street were sisters.

This building was later owned by Emma Lou Jordan in the late 1950s, who likewise lived on the first floor and rented rooms on the second floor until 1992.[54]

---

[54]Rhonda Jordan Haynes: Louella Isaac Jackson; Marie Walden Woodard; George Hill; Ethel Davis Blake; Habibullah Mujahid.

Eddie and Ola Mae Robinson
343 Palm Street
New Smyrna Beach, FL

This building was the business of Eddie and Ola Mae Robinson. They were the owners and operators of a juke joint in the 1940s; years later it became a store and was in operation well into the early 1970s. Ola Mae was the aunt of Lee Woulard Horne, wife of Roosevelt Horne a local building contractor and night club owner.[55]

---

[55]Marie Walden Woodard; Billy (Bo) Graham; Sandra Woodard.

Dr. George T. and Candice McDaniel
317 Sheldon Street
New Smyrna Beach, FL

Born in 1883, less than 20 years after slavery, George was a second generation post-slavery business owner. He built a home in New Smyrna, around the mid 1920s. Being a Negro physician he performed medical care for the Negro community, at a time when practicing medicine on any other race of people was not done in the south. He had a office on Washington Street, and he worked out of his home as needed and especially in times of emergencies. Dr. McDaniel's step-daughter Marion Jackson operated a beauty shop which can still be seen today located behind the house on the same property. [56]

---

[56]Louella Isaac Jackson; Marie Walden Woodard; Ethel Davis Blake: Annie Mae Bell.

Marion's Beauty Shop
317 Sheldon Street
New Smyrna Beach, FL

This building the Beauty Shop is located behind Dr. McDaniel's house at 317 Sheldon Street. It was operated by Marion Jackson, the daughter of Mrs. Candice McDaniel the second wife of Dr. McDaniel.[57]

---

[57]Louella Isaac Jackson; Marie Walden Woodard; Blake: Annie Mae Bell.

Cook Rooming House and Beauty Shop
Jordan Rooming House
336 Sheldon Street
New Smyrna Beach, FL

In the 1930 this two story luxurious rooming house was owned and operated by Mary Cook, mother of Willie Mae Green and George Cook. In 1950 Willie Mae Green operated a beauty parlor in the back of the house downstairs on the first floor. This property also contained a garage apartment and a single family home.

Years later, Leandrus and Novella Jordan, son and daughter-in-law of Carlus and Emma Lou Jordan owned and operated this sixteen room two-story rooming house from 1959 until around the mid 1970s. The renters were workers from the railroad and shrimp boats industries. Leandrus was the first black man in New Smyrna to run for a City Commission seat.[58]

---

[58]Rhonda Jordan Haynes: Polk City Directory 1950.

Burkey and Pearl Henderson Williams Morris
Ingham Road
New Smyrna Beach, FL

Pearl was a true business woman in her own right, at the age of 19, she already owned and operated a grocery store. The store was built around 1934 by her father Henry Harry Henderson, and was located on property near Ingham Road and State Road 44, not far from where her residence is today. The building was two stories, on the first floor was the grocery store and the family lived on the second floor. The store burned down in 1936 and was never rebuilt. Afterwards she became manager of a party house that had been a former funeral home. In 1936 Burkey and Pearl married and started a family. Then in 1940 they bought a boat and went in business as shrimp suppliers until 1942. According to local accounts they were the one and only black shrimp boat owners in Volusia County Florida during that period. A few years later they owned a house on South Myrtle Avenue that was converted in to apartments for girls.[59]

Henry Harry and Hattie Henderson
Ingham Road
New Smyrna Beach, FL

In the 1920s, 30s, and 40s Henry and Hattie Henderson owned and operated a dairy farm, milk was sold wholesale and retail; and they had a vegetable farm and sold vegetables door to door. The vegetable and dairy farm had large acreage that extended across highway 44, southward up Ingham Road and on Walden Street quite a ways. In addition to being, a farmer Henry was a Baptist minister, and a house builder.[60]

---

[59]Pearl Henderson Williams Morris; Robert (R.C.) Thompson; Pearlie Mae Morris Thompson.
[60]Pearl Henderson Williams Morris.

Courtesy of Rhonda Jordan Haynes

Mr. Carlus Jordan making his rounds at the gas station.

Courtesy Service Station and Garage
515 Avenue
New Smyrna Beach, FL

Sometime between the 1930s and 40s Carlus Jordan father of Leandrus Jordan, was the first black man to own a full services gas station in New Smyrna Beach, Florida.

In the 1940s and 50s Inez Brooks leased this Richfield gas station, it had a store and gas pumps, a garage and machine shop. She rented the garage and machine shop to John (J.W.) Lowery, until he was able to secure land and build his own station at 1501 Enterprise Avenue.

Years later this filling station was operated by other including a Mr. Canady, and Jenkins and Son in 1975, also for a short time it was a car dealership.

Today it is the location of "Lil Pop's" Professional Auto Detailing.[61]

---

[61]Louella Jackson; Marie Woodard; Rhonda Jordan Haynes.

Davis Store and Rooming House
Bookhart Four Point Grocery and Ice Cream Parlor
526 Mary Avenue
New Smyrna Beach, FL

This two-story building had a rooming house upstairs and a store down stairs. Fleming and Emily Rebecca Davis operated this business in the 1920s until sometime in the 1940s. Around the late 1940s and 50s John and Maude Bookhart operated Bookhart's Four Point Grocery and later a Ice Cream Parlor.[62]

Marie Walden Woodard Beauty Shop
539 Mary Avenue
New Smyrna Beach, FL

Mrs. Woodard started out as a beautician at Mrs. Rogers Shop, and later when she and husband James built the house she currently lives in they added a beauty shop on the northwest end of the home.[63]

Hattie Huff
Local Midwife
Lake Helen, FL

Hattie Huff, aunt of George Hill, John Windom, and grandmother of Leroy Lane, in the 1930s throughout the 50's was one of the local midwives that delivered babies in both the black and white communities (Cow Creek, New Smyrna, Oak Hill, Lake Helen, Deland, etc.,) in Volusia County as well as other nearby cities in Central Florida.[64]

---

[62]Louella Isaac Jackson; Ethel Davis Blake; Polk's City Directory 1950-1954.
[63]Marie Walden Woodard; Sandra Woodard; Corzet Lawrence.
[64]George Hill, Leroy Lane; Dorothy Nance Hill.

72

Lydia Pettis

Lydia Pettis operated a rooming house in her home on the southwest corner of Mary and Myrtle (today that location is the parking lot for Mount Olive Primitive Baptist Church.) In the 1940s she operated a restaurant at 539 Washington Street, that same building today sets next door and to the west of Manuel Franklin's OK Barber Shop.

Lydia started a program called the Forgotten Christmas Tree, where each year she would personally make sure the elderly and young persons in the community that had not received gifts for Christmas received something on (December 26) the day after Christmas.

Pettis Park on Mary Avenue and the southwest corner of North Duss Street, a few door over from her former residents was named in her honor "Pettis Park", as well as Pettis Court located on the south side of the Minerva Center going east from Myrtle Avenue to Palm Street.

The City also recognized Lydia for the work she performed in the community. At New Smyrna Beach City Hall, 210 Sams Avenue, just south of the front step lay a memorial stone in her honor. She was a true humanitarian and was well respected by all in the community.[65]

---

[65]Zeb Russell; George Manuel Franklin; Montez Nixon James.

Wilda Daniels Kindergarten
509 Josie Street
New Smyrna Beach, FL

Before there was an official kindergarten requirement, Mrs. Wilda Daniels operated a kindergarten in an orange grove near the old Alonzo "Babe" James Center on Washington Street, from there she moved the Kindergarten into a building on the corner of Mary and Josie Street sometime before 1950, today a park is located there on that property. The same building used for the kindergarten could be rented by members of the community for parties and other gatherings. [66]

Zeke and Rosa Wilson
State Road 44
New Smyrna Beach, FL

Zeke (Z W.) and Rosa Wilson owned a gas station and television repair shop from the late 1960 to early 1980. This was a full service station, offering gasoline, mechanic service, oil and tire changes, in addition to television repairs. The old building was situated on the southwest corner of Mission Road and State Road 44 and was still standing in the late 1990s. Today Walgreen Drug Store is located on the same property. [67]

---

[66]Louella Isaac Jackson; Ross Durham; Willie Mae Hill; Marie Walden Woodard.
[67]Ross Durham; James Hudson Sr.

Richard and Laura Hutchins
813 Hamilton Street
New Smyrna Beach, FL

Richard was self employed as a plaster part-time and worked on the police force full-time. He had also owned and operated Busy Bee Cab; as well the restaurant in the 1950s; years later from the 1980s until 2003 he sold fish door to door in Oak Hill, New Smyrna, Daytona, and Holly Hill, he was referred to as "The Fish Man." Laura worked outside the home as well as assisted with the businesses when time permitted.[68]

---

[68]Laura Hutchins; Roosevelt Horne; James Hudson, Sr.: George Hill.

CJT Beauty Shop
115 South Orange Avenue
New Smyrna Beach, FL

William and Mary Rollins owned and operated several businesses from the 1950s through the early 2000s. William worked for Florida East Coast Railroad for approximately 50 years before his retirement. Mary started working as a beautician in the 1950s out of Louise Rogers Beauty Shop on Washington Street. Also, William, Mary, and daughter Cassandra Singletary, owned and operated the Busy Bee Cab Service. In the early 1990s Mary's beauty shop (CJT) was located at 115 Orange Avenue; she worked there until her retirement in the early 2000s. Today this building houses Southern Instruments. [69]

---

[69]George Manuel Franklin; Laura Hutchins; Roosevelt Horne; Fannie Minson Hudson.

Guinn and Hives Concrete
Spruce Street
New Smyrna Beach, FL

Walter Guinn and Jimmy Lee Hives, started this father and son concrete finishing team in 1969; concrete work done included digging building footer, laying out floor foundations, and pouring concrete floor slabs. In 1973 the partnership was dissolved, and both Walter and Jimmy Lee started their own businesses. Walter and Effie Guinn owned and operated their concrete business from 19731991. Jimmie Lee and Eurcell (Jackie) Hives started Hives Concrete in 1973 and was in operation until 1988.[70]

Pearson Photography and Beauty Shop
Palm Street
New Smyrna Beach, FL

He was handsome, she was pretty. He was a sharp dresser, she was a sharper dresser. He had a photograph studio in the home; she had a beauty shop in the home too. James and Marilyn Pearson were an example of the successful young couples. Boys wanted to be like James, and girls wanted to be like Marilyn. James took pictures and Marilyn did hair in the 1950s and 60s, their skills were sought after by people in the community and surrounding towns, their appointment calendar for services were always filled to capacity, sometime people would be waiting in line begging for an appointment to get one or another of their services.[71]

---

[70]Jimmie Hives.
[71]James Hudson, Sr.

Henry J. and Ophelia Rainge
406 South Duss Street
New Smyrna Beach, FL

Henry J. and Ophelia Rainge operated several businesses from their home, in addition to Henry J. working 51 years for the railroad. Their first business was a commercial laundry on their back porch in 1950, sporting nine commercial bendex washers and four dryers. Next, in 1957 they purchased a taxicab franchise from Edith and Mallie Whitehead. Their taxicab fleet contained six new automobiles, providing fares for both the black and white sections of town. Finally, in the mid 1960s they had a chicken farm, raised chickens in their back yard, and when full grown fresh chickens could be purchased for 20 cents per pound.[72]

---

[72]Ophelia Rainge; Ralph Rainge; George Manuel Franklin.

79

Reliable Cleaners
104 Orange Avenue
New Smyrna Beach, FL

Wallace and Annie Mitchell owned a tailor shop and pressing club (dry cleaners) in the 1930s on the southwest corner of Julia and Dimmick Street; and in the 1940s his pressing club was located here at 104 North Orange Avenue.[73]

---

[73]Willie Mae Meeks Hill; Chanel Mitchell.

Courtesy of Rhonda Jordan Haynes

Engrahm Hotel
Bethune Beach Casino
New Smyrna Beach, FL

In the 1940s George Engrahm owned at least three businesses on Bethune Beach (named after Dr. Mary McLeod Bethune) in New Smyrna on the Atlantic Ocean, the only beach accessible to Blacks in Volusia County, until around the 1970s. Some of the businesses he owned were a bar (for adults only) a long one story motel on the beach, and a place for teenagers where they could dance and purchase ice cream, potato chips, cookies, candies ,etc.

Local legend has it that Joe Louis the world famous boxing champion at one time owned that same motel and was frequently in New Smyrna training and sparring.

Sometime in the 1980s the motel and other business were torn down and replaced with condominiums and other named living accommodations.

It was also stated that George Engrahm at one time owned the building that housed the old Central Bar at 519 Julia Street.

Leandrus Jordan, son of Carlus and Emma Lou also operated this adult social club in the 1960, which was called the Bethune Beach Casino.[74]

---

[74]Johnny Thomas; George Hill; Roosevelt Horne; Rhonda Jordan Haynes.

The United States of America.

CERTIFICATE
No. 9036 } To all to whom these presents shall come, Greeting:

Whereas, *Leroy Chisholm of Volusia County Florida*

has deposited in the GENERAL LAND OFFICE of the United States a Certificate of the Register of the Land Office at *Gainesville Florida* whereby it appears that full payment has been made by the said *Leroy Chisholm* according to the provisions of the Act of Congress of the 24th of April, 1820, entitled "An Act making further provision for the sale of the Public Lands," and the acts supplemental thereto, for *the north east quarter of section twenty five in township eighteen south of range thirty east of Tallahassee Meridian in Florida Containing one hundred and fifty nine acres and seventy four hundredths of an acre*

according to the official plat of the survey of the said lands returned to the General Land Office by the Surveyor General, which said tract has been purchased by the said *Leroy Chisholm*

Now know ye, That the United States of America, in consideration of the premises, and in conformity with the several acts of Congress in such case made and provided, HAVE GIVEN AND GRANTED, and by these presents DO GIVE AND GRANT, unto the said *Leroy Chisholm*

and to *his* heirs the said tract above described: To have and to hold the same, together with all the rights, privileges, immunities, and appurtenances, of whatsoever nature, thereunto belonging, unto the said *Leroy Chisholm*

and to *his* heirs and assigns forever.

In testimony whereof, I *Grover Cleveland*

PRESIDENT OF THE UNITED STATES OF AMERICA, have caused these letters to be made patent, and the seal of the General Land Office to be hereunto affixed.

Given under my hand, at the City of Washington, the *third* day of *June*, in the year of our Lord one thousand eight hundred and *eighty five*, and of the Independence of the United States the one hundred and *ninth*.

By the President: *Grover Cleveland*
By *M. Hoff*, Secretary.
N. C. ___ Recorder of the General Land Office.

Courtesy Bureau of Land Management -General Land Office Records

Mr. Leroy Chisholm, pioneer, barber, businessman, and humanitarian, was born during slavery, around 1858; and he was a land owner in 1885 at the age of 27, approximately 22 years after slavery. He owned 159+ acres of land in Volusia County Florida; this property was believed to have been located some where between Debary and New Smyrna.

In 1900 Mr. Leroy Chisholm resided in New Smyrna. It was stated that even though he had acquired land and had a house on Riverside Drive, know as Hillsborough Avenue in those days, his front door was nailed shut by persons in the community, who demanded and made sure that he could only used the back door of his residence to enter and exit his home. Compliance with this demand was ensured by threats on life and property.

Leroy was the proprietor of a barbershop on Canal Street some time in the early 1900s. He was also reported to have owned a two story building on the corner of Dimmick and Washington Street, one of the reported tenants in that build during the mid 1920s was a local black physician named Dr. Thomas McDaniel.

Chisholm Academy, later Chisholm High School, (all black schools during segregation) and the current Chisholm Elementary Schools located on Ronnoc Lane were all named in honor of the late Mr. Leroy Chisholm[75]

---

[75]Willie Mae Meeks Hill;. Florida Bureau of Land Management.

Cut Masters
715 Canal Street
New Smyrna Beach, FL

From the early 1990s to the mid 1990s Derrick and Darcia Warthaw Harris, owned and operated Cut Masters, a beauty and barber shop in this building on Canal Street. During that time their business was the only black owned combination beauty and barber shop west of the railroad tracks. This shop boasted six work stations, four shampoo stations, and four hair drying stations, a barber station, and a nail technician station. Beauticians (Cosmetologists) were Darcia Warthaw Harris, Vicki Durham, Wanda Walker; and others working there at that time were Derrick Harris, barber; and Fannie Minson Hudson, esthetician and nail technician. Today this building houses the WIC Store[76]

---

[76] Derrick and Darcia Warthaw Harris; Wanda Walker; Fannie Minson Hudson; Vicki Durham.

Wadley Beauty Shop
700 Canal Street
New Smyrna Beach, FL

Vicki Wadley was owner and operator of Wadley Beauty Shop in the late 1980s and early 1990s. She was the first beautician to bring new chemical products for the black hair to the other black beauticians in this area. This build was also the home base for Zow Security Services from mid 1990s until 2005. Zow Security Services were owned and operated by Sam and Katherine Wadley Zow, the brother-in-law and sister of Vicki Wadley.[77]

[77]Katherine Wadley Zow; Fannie Minson Hudson.

86

Carter Fruit and Produce
Roper Street
New Smyrna Beach, FL

Earnest Carter a self employed farmer, lived on the southwest corner of Roper and Brooks Streets. He grew vegetable, fruits, and raised hogs and cows. He was still farming, and selling produce and live stock in early 1980. The lot where his home once stood is vacant today.[78]

Conyers Convenience Store
Oak Street
New Smyrna Beach, FL

Jody Conyers, Sr., had a convenience store on the southeast corner of Enterprise Avenue and Oak Street. The store sold cookies, candies, drinks, and ice cream.[79]

Annie Logan
Sheldon Street
New Smyrna Beach, FL

Annie Logan, a beautician worked out of her home on Sheldon Street near where Allen Chapel AME Church is located today. Annie was the sister of Parker Meeks, the owner of a grocery store at 440 Myrtle Avenue in the 1920s.[80]

---

[78]Fannie Hudson; Peter Carl Shedrick.
[79]Fannie Hudson; Peter Carl Shedrick.
[80]Marie Walden Woodard

Rogers' Wood-yard
516 Ronnoc Lane
New Smyrna Beach, FL

Clarence Rogers, father of Gordon Sr., and Arzy Rogers, owned a wood-yard in the 1930s, in addition to working for the Florida East Coast Railroad. He owned two trucks used for hauling the wood, and employed two men to deliver wood throughout the community. Wood was used as fuel, for heating the home, for cooking, and used to boil white clothing clean before hanging them up to dry.[81]

TAXI CAB COMPANIES

Florence Brown was the first black female taxicab owner in New Smyrna.[82]

Sammie Graham, Taxi Company was located behind Bookhart's Ice Cream Parlor on the corner of Mary Avenue and Palm Street, and was in operation from the mid 1950 until about 1965.[83]

Lester and Annie Mae Mitchell owed a taxi company from the late 1960s to early 1970.[84]

Charles Smith (grandfather of Brenda, Fred, Lawrence, and Lorenzo Thompson) owned a taxicab company.[85]

Mallie and Edith Whitehead, owned a taxicab franchise, later sold it to Henry J. Rainge.[86]

---

[81]Arzy Rogers; Gordon Rogers. Jr.
[82]Ethel Davis Blake: Allen Chapel Mens' Day Committee.
[83]George Manuel Franklin; Roosevelt Horne.
[84]George Manuel Franklin; Chanel Mitchell.
[85]George Manuel Franklin.
[86]Ralph Rainge; Ophelia Rainge.

1885 Black Business Owners

Bolden, F., farmer[87]

1900 Black Business Owners

Bert, James, barber
Glover, Lewis, barber
Little, Lawrence, house painter
Morgan, Ben, printer
Morgan, Mary, artist[88]
Powell, Henry, carpenter
Singleton, Richard, upholster
?, George, tailor

1910 Black Business Owners

Brown, William, mason
Davis, Edward, carpenter
Davis, Mary, dressmaker
Harper, Ketura, boarding house owner
Howard, Jennie, dress maker
Little, James, self-employed brick mason. 1910-1920, self-employed plasterer in 1930
Livingston, David, carpenter
Strod, Birch, carpenter
Williams, Louise, boarding house owner[89]

---

[87]Florida State Census: 1885
[88]Florida State Census: 1900
[89]Florida State Census: 1910

1920 Black Business Owners

Brooks, John, carpenter
Cook, Mary, restaurant owner
Felton, Mamie, hairdresser
Larkin, Henry, grocery store owner
Little, James, self-employed brick mason 1910-1920, self-employed plasterer in 1930.
Masters, Willie, restaurant owner
Meeks, Oscar and Anna May Meeks, own tailor shop and dry cleaners in 1920 and 30s.
Mizell, Charles and Mattie, farmers 1920, and a self-employed dairyman 1930.
Moody, Julia, restaurant owner
Nelson, Sy, restaurant owner
Newkirk, James and Percilla, restaurant owner
Owens, Henry and Pearl, poolroom owner
Page, Peter, restaurant owner
Peterson, Raymond, own clothing shop
Robinson, John and Belle Robinson, barber shop owner Smithon, Alley and Galetha Smithon, barber shop owner Woodard, Julia, restaurant owner[90]

---

[90]United State Census: 1920.

1930 Black Business Owners

Cook, Mary, rooming house owner
Davis, Clinton and Daisy, café owner
Evans, Henrietta, rooming house owner
Franklin, James and Mattie, merchant fish market
Jones, Ernest, café owner
Little, James, self-employed brick mason 1910-1920, self-employed plasterer in 1930.
McDaniel, George, physician
McLendon, Elgin, carpenter
McLendon, L.G., carpenter
McLendon, Lelah, dressmaker
Moody, Nora, dressmaker
Patterson, Leona, rooming house owner
Pearson, Nora, dressmaker
Powell, Mary, café owner
Ronae, Ceagan, and Alexzena, poolroom owner
Smithton, Alley, barber shop owner
Stewart, Viney, owner, boarding house owner
Thompson, Edgar, café owner
Tucker, John, barber shop owner
Walker, Joseph, and Ophelia, café owner
Washington, George, painter
Watson, Corrine, boarding house owner
Watson, John and Mina, store owner
Williams, Sarah, and Chip, café owner
Williams, Willie, pressman, shop owner[91]

---

[91]United State Census: 1930.

TERMS

Adult Social Club -A place where people met to socialize, have a few drinks, converse to unwind after a busy work day.

Boarding house where individuals received meals in addition to occupying a room, sometimes laundry service was provided as well. Sharecropper/Farmers -men and their families working the farms of others were called sharecroppers. Many times after the landowners got their split of the crop there was nothing left for the sharecropper.

Laundress/Washerwoman-women provided laundry services from their homes.

Rooming house -where individuals lived and were responsible for getting their own meals.

QUESTION AND ANSWER

Question: Were there black people in New Smyrna, Florida, before homes and business were recorded west of the railroad tracks?

Answer: Yes.

BUSINESSES

OF

THE

PRESENT

Before

2006 Bethel Baptist Church New Smyrna Beach, Florida

After

James Hudson, Sr., is a third generation master plasterer, his father and grandfather were plasterers. He has 30+ years experience doing residential, commercial, and church plastering.

James' area of expertise is stucco, imitation brick and stones work, synthetic application system, dry wall, and repair work. He owns and operates the business.

James and wife Fannie reside in New Smyrna Beach, FL.[92]

HUDSON PLASTERING SERVICE, INC.
699 West Street
New Smyrna Beach, FL 32168
Phone: (386)427-6270
Cell: (386)290-3306

When you want your plastering done correct, Call us we have experience and respect.

---

[92]James Hudson, Sr.; Fannie Minson Hudson.

(2006-Outside view) Boat Dock -Anglers Club-New Smyrna Beach, Florida)

(2006-Inside view 1) Boat Dock -Anglers Club-New Smyrna Beach, Florida)

(2006-Inside view 2) Boat Dock -Anglers Club-New Smyrna Beach, Florida)

96

James (Jim) and Debbie Marcisak Brendel own and operate J. Brendel Enterprises, Inc. They specialize in commercial and residential building, and marine dock construction.

Jim is a state certified residential and commercial contractor with more than 20 years experience in the field. In addition to constructing new buildings, Jim does repair work, renovations and restorations of buildings and boat docks. Jim and Debbie are the parents of two loving adult daughters and grandparents of two adorable little girls.

Jim and wife Debbie reside in New Smyrna Beach, FL.[93]

J. BRENDEL ENTERPRISES, INC.
1801 N. Peninsula Avenue
New Smyrna Beach, FL
Phone (386)428-5715
Cell (386)426-3979

To want quality work in a hurry is not a crime,
Call Jim, he will get it done right and on time.

---

[93]James (Jim) Brendel. Debbie Marcisak Brendel.

Willie Woods Masonry is owned and operated by Willie and Harriet Woods. Willie is a hands on boss, and is very customer oriented. He has more than 20 years experience doing masonry work in the Volusia County Area. "I feel experience and giving the customer what they want is the difference between another job done, and a great job done for a satisfied customers." Willie and wife Harriet reside in Oak Hill, FL.[94]

"WILLIE WOODS MASONRY"
200 Cypress Avenue

Oak Hill, FL (386)345-2776

For your masonry work done just right,
Call Willie, he will get it right if it takes all night.

Vern Brown Automotive Repair Shop has been a part of the Westside neighborhood for more than 25 years. It does not matter if it is day or night when a call for service come in, Vern will make sure that caller get the same quality services as the next customer in the door. "A man's word is his bond, if you say you are going to do something, do it." Vern and wife Bernice live in New Smyrna Beach, FL.[95]

VERN BROWN AUTOMOTIVE REPAIR SHOP
409 Warren Avenue
New Smyrna Beach, FL (386) 427-3012

For supreme motor vehicle care and repairs in this town,
Visit Vern Brown for a job done remarkably well the first go-around.

---

[94]Willie A. Woods.
[95]Vern Brown; Fannie Hudson.

Donald T. Bell, son of retired railroad engineer and builder Warrnon Bell, and former City Commissioner Oretha Wyche Bell. Donald is a Vietnam War Veteran and recipient of the Bronze Star, was one of the two first black men (the other was Michael Williams) from New Smyrna Beach in 1969 to work for corporate America.

He is a retired sales and marketing (guru) executive, worked for General Foods, Maxwell House Coffee, and M&M Mars for a total of 36 years before retiring.

Donald is a one-man band and continues to wears many professional and volunteer service hats. He is a builder since 1982, a Realtor since 2004, an Insurance Agent since 2004, and worldwide Youth Mentor since 1973.

Following in his parents footsteps is not an option for Donald but an opportunity and honor. He loving smiles and stated "I guess the legacy my parents started years ago will have to be carried on by me because they won't take no for an answer."
"My parents are my superheroes, they taught me well, and are still teaching me to be the best that I can at whatever task I undertake. My other mentor Mr. Howard Loveless (now deceased) our neighbor taught me about treating others fair, about self confidence, and about salesmanship.

It is because of my parents and Mr. Howard Loveless, that I am who I am today. As a kid I had the best of both worlds, so there was no way for me to miss the mark. Every time I give something back to the youth I mentor worldwide I think of the three people who gave me a start in life."

Donald, wife Lucy and son Sheldon reside in Ormond Beach, FL.[96]

INNER-CITY ENTERPRISES
119 Buckskin Lane
Ormond Beach, FL
(386)405-7511

---

[96]Donald Bell; Warrnon Bell, Sr.; Oretha Wyche Bell; Montez Nixon James.

Between the 1930s and 40s Carlus Jordan father of Leandrus Jordan, owned and operated a gas station at this address. He was the first black man to own a full service gas station on the Westside of New Smyrna Beach.

Then in the 1940s and 1950s Inez Brooks operated the gas station and store, and John (J.W.) Lowery rented and operated the garage and machine shop.

Today Cornelius (Lil Pop) Mitchell, son of Willie (Pop) Mitchell, owns and operates "Lil Pop's" Professional Auto Detailing at this location. He is a native of New Smyrna Beach, FL, and has been performing magic on driving machines in the same location for the last 5 years.[97]

"LIL POP'S" PROFESSIONAL AUTO DETAILING
515 Mary Avenue
New Smyrna Beach, FL

To get the best cleaned and greatest smelling driving machine,
Come see "Lil Pop" you will see what I mean.

---

[97]Cornelius Mitchell.; Pete Tindle, Rhonda Jordan Haynes.

101

Neal (Lil Neal) Coates Jr., son of Neal (Big Neal) and Laura Coates, makes the best bar-b-que you will ever put in your mouth. He is a true old-school proprietor; he worked his way up from the bottom of his own bar-b-que business. He sold bar-b-que on the roadside, at special events, in addition to catering private parties and events. Today he is owner and operator of "Lil Neal's BBQ located on one of the busiest highways (Business State Road 44 also know as Canal Street) in East Central Florida. Neal and wife Kelley and their children reside in New Smyrna Beach, FL.[98]

LIL' NEAL'S BBQ
1112 Canal Street (State Road 44)
New Smyrna Beach, FL 32168
(386)428-2864

The best Bar-B-Que in these parts of the
south,
Come on by Lil' Neal's you will be so glad you trusted
your mouth.

---

[98]Neal Coates, Jr.

Charles and Marvalyn Mathis own and operate Tamishco, Inc. They started this business to help fulfill a life long vision of helping those less fortunate than themselves, as well as a way to give something back to the community they love so much. In addition, Charles is a minister and an employee of Florida Power Lights. Charles, Marvalyn, and son Marquis reside in New Smyrna Beach, FL.[99]

TAMISHCO, INC.
440 Julia Street
New Smyrna Beach, FL 32168
(386)428-2923

Need a job or a place to stay,
Call Charles and Marvalyn and watch blessings
come your way.

---

[99]Charles Mathis; Marvalyn Mathis.

Darrell and Dwayne Jones have been around landscaping work most of their lives. They actually knew about landscaping before starting first grade, because they would follow their father to work most days. You can say they were born into it and taught by the best, their father, Mr. Earl Jones, Sr., a master landscaper. Both Darrell and Dwayne their wives and children reside in New Smyrna Beach, FL.[100]

JONES AND JONES LANDSCAPING
477 Oak Street
New Smyrna Beach, FL 32168
(386)314-9348

For landscaping that is by far superior,
Call Jones & Jones Landscaping to beautify
your exterior.

---

[100]Darrell Jones; Dwayne Jones.

Built in 1952 this location was the full service gas station and garage owned and operated by John (J. W.) and Annie Lowery. Years later, in the 1970s and 80s Neal (Big Neal) and Laura Coates operated a auto-body shop at this address.

Today, this building is the business place of Airport Auto Air & Service, owned and operated by Guy Clements and John Wooten. They have a combined 65+ years experience in auto repair and maintenance.

For the past 19 years, they have performed car care magic right here in New Smyrna Beach. Airport Auto Air specializes in air condition repair, brake replacement, water pump removal and replacements, and general auto repair. It is the only auto air and repair services on the west side of New Smyrna Beach.

The owners take pride in performing work that exceeds the Automotive Service of Excellence Certification guidelines. "Honesty and great work is our stance".[101]

AIRPORT AUTO AIR & SERVICE
1501 Enterprise Avenue
New Smyrna Beach, FL 32168
(386)423-3169 or (386)428-5586

To get your auto air conditioner fix, or brake work done with flair, or for other general auto repairs at a price that   is fair,

Come by see Wally, John, and Guy at Airport   Auto Air.

---

[101]Guy Clements; John Wooten.

Patricia Plummer Gaskin is owner and operator of Miss "P" Hair Designs. She is a native of Oak Hill, Florida; and has had her beauty salon open in the same location for the past 10 years. Patricia has been providing first-rate hair care, beauty treatments, and nail care for over 20 years, she specializes in weaves, perms, relaxers and cuts. Patricia and husband Gregory reside in Port Orange, FL.[102]

MISS "P" HAIR DESIGNS
2102 South Ridgewood Avenue, Unit 27
Edgewater, FL 32141
(386) 409-7525

For hair designs that have no equal and are beyond compare,
Stop by and see Miss "P". She will do wonders for your hair.

---

[102]Patricia Plummer Gaskin.

Arthur "Art" Williams is a second generation tree service craftsman. His father Arthur "Big John" Williams, taught him at an early age the skills and self confidence needed for the trade. Today, Art is owner and operator of Williams Tree Service, with 40+ years experience providing expert tree service. Art and wife Russelle reside in New Smyrna Beach, FL.[103]

WILLIAMS TREE SERVICE
473 Spruce Street
New Smyrna Beach, FL 32168
(386)423-3616

For tree removal, limb pruning, and a wide-range of
tree care,
Call Art for a job expertly done, and some
laughs to share.

---

[103]Arthur (Art) Williams; Russelle Williams.

Warrnon and Oretha Wyche Bell are owners of Southern Oaks Town Houses, the first and only black owned housing establishment of this caliber in New Smyrna Beach.

Warrnon a WWII Veteran, a retired builder, a former railroad fireman, and retired railroad Engineer for Florida East Coast Railroad with 38 years of service, was one of the first group of three black men in New Smyrna Beach working for Florida East Coast Railroad in the 1950s to take and pass the railroad engineer examination to become an engineer.

Oretha the first black female Airplane Mechanic from New Smyrna Beach during WWII, a retired educator, and the first black female to become City Commissioner in New Smyrna Beach, retained the office of Commissioner District 4 for a total of 15 years before retiring from public service.

For Warrnon and Oretha, the vision for Southern Oaks housing complex grew out of a passion and commitment to help others as well as provide affordable housing for the less fortunate and deserving members of the Westside community. To help keep that dream alive they assist those in need with quality affordable rental housing at under market prices. Warrnon and wife Oretha reside in New Smyrna Beach, FL.[104]

Southern Oaks
611-620 Warn-Ree Circle
New Smyrna Beach, FL

Courtesy of Oretha Wyche Bell

---

[104]Warrnon Bell, Sr.; Oretha Wyche Bell; Montez Nixon James.

The Lowery Brown Apartments located at 436 Myrtle Avenue, were built sometime around 1920, and has served as home and rooming house, Chapel, as well as a community center.

In the late 1980s the building was rehabilitated and refurbished, today it severs as a duplex apartment building. Each apartment consist of three bedrooms, a kitchen, a bath, and generous onsite parking. The apartments are owned and managed by Alphonso and Dorothy Lowery Brown, and daughter Pamela A. Brown.

The Brown's have a combined 80+ years experience in the service and public service areas; Mr. Brown now retired worked 32+ years at Kennedy Space Center, working his way up from custodian to project manager.

Mrs. D. Brown a retired educator has 37½ years teaching and advising experience, in addition to 5 years experiences as a daycare consultant; and Ms. P. Brown putting her life on hold provided care for her ailing grandfather until his demise some 4 years later, today she works with Volusia County Public Schools as a special educations teacher.[105]

LOWERY BROWN APARTMENTS
436 Myrtle Avenue
New Smyrna Beach, FL 32168

[105]Dorothy Lowery Brown; United States Census 1930; Volusia County Clerk of Courts 1925; Volusia County Property Appraiser 1925-1930; Montez Nixon James.

Howard is owner and operator of Howard Teemer Painting. He has been doing superb interior and exterior painting on houses, and commercial building for more than 30 years. In addition to being a painter Howard is a veteran of the United States Armed Forces, a minister of the Gospel, the son of Minister Doley Teemer (deceased), and nephew of Reverend Thomas Teemer. Howard and wife Edna reside in New Smyrna Beach, FL.[106]

HOWARD TEEMER PAINTING
801 West Street
New Smyrna Beach, FL
(386)428-9645

For painting that looks good and is carefree for a longtime,
Phone Howard for painting that lasts come rain or shine.

---

[106]Howard Teemer; Edna Teemer.

2006-Window Tinting at Bethel Baptist Church, New Smyrna Beach, FL.

John and Laura Montisano, own and operate Energy Guard a solar window tinting business. Laura has 25+ years experience doing this type work and enjoys helping others. "You have to love what you do, and you have to love people." Energy Guard specializes in window and door tinting for the home, business, and place of worship. Laura and husband John reside in Daytona Beach, FL.[107]

ENERGY GUARD
1575 Aviation Parkway Ct. #516
Daytona Beach, FL 32114
(386)253-3000

Don't let the cost of your heating and electric bill
get you down,
Call Laura at Energy Guard she will help you
save money all year around.

---

[107]Laura Montisano.

114

Sam and Katharine Wadley Zow, are owners of A Quest for Knowledge Learning Center, a place for preschool learning and growth. Jennifer Waters, daughter-in-law of Sam and Katherine is director and manager of the center. Katherine a retired Professional Registered Nurse started this business in 1990 to help little ones learn, learn, and learn. Sam and Katharine, and daughter-in-law Jennifer reside in New Smyrna Beach, FL.[108]

A QUEST FOR KNOWLEDGE LEARNING CENTER
829 Canal Street
New Smyrna Beach, FL 32168
(386) 428-8841

For loving and secure child care that leaves no doubt,
Send your child to Jennifer, love, care and security is what she is all about.

---

[108]Katharine Wadley Zow; Jennifer Waters.

115

Lavelle Waters is owner of Waters Funeral Services, and has been providing caring funeral preparations, cremation, and burial services in New Smyrna Beach, for the past four years. Lavell and wife Jennifer are the son and daughter-in-law of Sam and Catherine Wadley Zow, owners of A Quest for Knowledge Learning Center, and Zow Security. Lavell and Jennifer reside in New Smyrna Beach, FL.[109]

WATERS FUNERAL SERVICES
414 Mary Avenue
New Smyrna Beach, FL 32168
(386)427-9366

When funeral arrangements and interment care is
a must,
Look to Waters Funeral Home for professional
services you can trust.

---

[109]Katharine Wadley Zow; Jennifer Waters.

George Manuel Franklin has been in the barbering and hair care business since 1948. He started out working at 215 Dimmick Street with Arthur Davis. Manuel received his barber training at McCoy Barber College in Chicago, IL, shortly after serving time in the Armed Forces. Today services include hair cuts, face massages, and mustache trims.. Manuel and wife Jinnie reside in New Smyrna Beach, FL.[110]

OK Barbershop
535 Washington Street
New Smyrna Beach, FL

For a magnificent hair cut or mustache trim fit for a king,
Go see Manuel, for a look that will make you smile and sing.

---

[110]George "Manuel" Franklin; Willie Mae Meeks Hill.

Calvin "Bear" White is owner and operator of Calvin White Masonry, LLC. He is a native of Oak Hill, FL, his family has lived in New Smyrna Beach off and on most of his life. He has many years experience doing masonry work, and takes pride in doing great work at a fair price. Calvin and wife Antoinette reside in New Smyrna Beach, FL. [111]

CALVIN "BEAR" WHITE MASONRY, LLC
603 North Duss Street
New Smyrna Beach, Fl 32169
(386)847-0578

For masonry work done with credibility, style, and finesse,
Call Calvin the "Bear" for great work at a price you can caress.

---

[111]Calvin "Bear" White.

Mark Bell is owner and operator of Green Machine Tree Service. He is a native Floridian, and a 1991 graduate of New Smyrna Beach High School. Mark has 10 years experience in the tree service, and provides a variety of tree and scrubby care, in addition to debris clean-up and removal.[112]

GREEN MACHINE TREE SERVICE

317 Inwood Avenue
New Smyrna Beach, FL
(386) 663-4309

For tree services that get attention and is a
beautiful sight,
Ask for Mark and watch your tree care worries
take flight.

---

[112]Mark Bell.

119

This build was first occupied by Smyrna Funeral Home, owned by Willis Settle and managed by Mildred Smith from the 1940s until the 1960s.

Sometime in the early 1970s Dr. Rabie Gainous owned and operated Gainous Funeral Homes in both New Smyrna Beach and in Daytona Beach.

Today Alexander Wynn III, owns and operates Gainous-Wynn Funeral Homes in Daytona Beach, and in New Smyrna Beach, FL.[113]

GAINOUS-WYNN FUNERAL HOME
570 Washington Street
New Smyrna Beach, FL 32168
(386)428-5751

In times of sorrow when you need a friend,
Remember to call on Gainous-Wynn.

---

[113]Johnny Thomas; George Manuel Franklin; George Hill; Dorothy Hill; Marie Walden Woodard.

120

Conclusion

It is a known fact that, not all slaves were blacks; not all blacks were slaves; some were born free, others bought their freedom, yet many more had no way out and remained slaves. This book is not a attempt to point fingers at anyone, neither to cause pain or shame, but to tell things as they really were and are today.

To help readers understand the purpose for this book, it must be shared that the accomplishments of the black people during these trying time (1800s and 1900s) was and still is a source of great of pride. The additional purpose for this book is to document the skills, services, ownership, and management of business, as well as other accomplishments of the negro people in America and New Smyrna, after the abolishment of slavery. In a short time and starting out with little or nothing they were able to achieve so much.

Just like the butterfly in the cocoon before metamorphosis, these great people attained in one or two generations what it has taken other cultures many generations to accomplish. For their courage, perseverance, love, and trust in God, I will be forever grateful.

Because of its historical contents every effort has been made to be as accurate as possible in sharing this experience about the people and businesses of the past as well as businesses in operation today. To that effect 99.999% of the data comes directly from the actual business owners, and persons interviewed who were present during the operation of these businesses, or family members, friends, and relatives of past and present business owners.

EASY

TO

MAKE AND COOK

SOUTHERN

STYLE

RECIPES

Southern style recipes are usually simple to make because the cook uses whatever ingredients already on hand. To help keep recipes in their original southern tradition some measurements are not given, and in addition recipes can be adjusted to fit any size group.

Cooking is an individual thing, and true cooking skills come from doing it over and over until the recipe comes out each time just the way the cook wants it to.

For working individuals it can be a gift not having to worry about cooking a nutritious meal everyday. Especially when s/he gets home tired or something comes up on short notice and s/he has to choose between eating fast food or nutritious good food.

Have no fear the cooking show starts here. The cook can have peace of mind, fun, and nutritious meal for one or two more days in the coming week.

HOW? On Saturday cook an extra large meal, pretend you are having company for dinner. The same things can be done for Sunday as well.

After dinner take the leftover and place them in a Entrée container and freeze it. Don't forget to label and date the containers.

Don't worry you can freeze almost anything and it will taste just as good if not better than it did the day it was cooked. However, I don't recommend keeping frozen leftovers for more than 1-2 months. If in doubt ask an experienced cook what s/he would do.

Hey Stouffer's and Mrs. Smith have taught us there is nothing like home cooking. Just look in the freezer section at the super market, there are all types of heat and eat foods, (full of sodium) waiting to be taken home to be reheated or micro-waved.

Now if the cook, were to cooked two days, there might be enough food left over for three or four meals for the coming week, leaving free time to do what you enjoy most. As a bonus eat out one night to reward yourself.

Hints:

For storing leftover foods in freezer, stock up on plastic reusable Glad or Zip-Lock Entree containers, as well as sandwich bags and gallon size freezer bags. Food containers and bags are rather inexpensive and can be purchased at most grocery and discount stores. The amount and types of leftover may vary, remember the objectives are to save time, money, and have nutritious meals.

Feedback on the recipes and hints is very much appreciated.

Sincerely,

Fannie Minson Hudson
699 West Street
New Smyrna Beach, FL 32168
Email: hnsbb@yahoo.com

Pan Cake Mix

If this is your first time making homemade pancakes, you are in for a real treat. This recipe makes enough pancake mix for four medium size pancakes or two large pancakes.

2-c. Self-Rising Flour

1-Egg

2-oz. Milk

1-tablespoon Cooking Oil (Vegetable, or Canola) Skillet

Mix flour and egg together.

Next, mix in milk slowly, you want batter to the consistency of cake batter.

If this is not enough milk, use a little more until you get the batter the way you want it.

Heat cooking oil in skillet, next pour in mix, repeat until you have used up all the batter.

Top pancakes with your favorite syrup.

Congratulation you are on your way to being a great chef.

Hush Puppy Mix

Self-Rising Flour
Self-Rising Cornmeal
Egg Milk Chopped onions
Whole Kernel Corn
Cooking Oil Vegetable or Canola
Fry Daddy
Tablespoon to pour batter

Make hushpuppy mixture of ½ flour and ½ corn meal; add eggs, chopped onions, and whole Kernel corn. Mix well, until the consistency of cake batter.

Heat cooking oil Fry Daddy or frying pan, or pot. When oil is ready use tablespoon to measure up hushpuppies, and drop it in the hot cooking oil.

Now all you need is some fish or collard greens and you will be eating Georgia style.

Sweet Potato Pie

Preheat Oven: 375

OK Children you know I don't make Pie Crust.
Winn Dixie, Publix, or Food Lion can do it.

Sweet Potato's boiled until tender.
When easy to pick up, pull off skin.
Mash Sweet Potatoes up real good.
Add, Nutmeg, Eggs, Sugar Cinnamon, Canned Milk,
Whole Milk and Butter.

Beat real good, taste as you go.

You know how it should taste, if it's good before it's done,
it will be good after.

I don't measure with Potato Pies, Momma does it
with Love and Soul.

**This recipe is from the book "Momma Lee Home
Cooking" by LeFonia McDaniels Boyd**

127

Hamburger Patties-James Style

Ground Chuck
Egg
Onions
Salt Pepper Bell pepper
Garlic (chopped or garlic powder)
Pam Spray
Hamburger presser (or do it the old fashion way use your hands)
Skillet

Take ½ of the ground chuck and place in bottom of mixing bowl or pan.

Add in egg, onion, salt, pepper, bell pepper, garlic.

Next place the other ½ of ground chuck in pan to make the top layer.

Use you hand to knead mixture until all ingredients are well mixed with the ground chuck.

Divided meat into equal parts. For example if you have 2 lbs of ground chuck divided it into eight (8) sections.

Take one section and place it in hamburger presser, or use you hand to make a **round or square** hamburger patty.

Spray Skillet with Pam spray; heat skillet on stove at medium heat.

When the skillet is hot enough to fry meat, place hamburger patty in skillet and cook until done.

Turkey Wings

Let's Talk TURKEY

Preheat Oven: 350

Season turkey wings with Seasoning Salt, Pepper, Accent, and Paprika.

Place the wings in a nice size roaster pan.

Cut up some Bell peppers & Onions, and spread the Onions and Bell peppers over the wings.

Melt 1-tablespoon of butter in about 2 oz of water, next pour this mixture on the turkey wings inside the roaster pan.

Finally, cover and bake until tender. Enjoy.

This recipe is from the book "Momma Lee Home Cooking" by LeFonia McDaniels Boyd

Stuffed Mushrooms

Mushrooms
Pam Cooking Spray
Crabmeat
1-Egg Mayonnaise
Onions Bread Crumbs (Progresso Italian Bread Crumbs)
Margarine
Baking Dish

Preheat oven: 350

Clean and wash mushrooms, remove stems.

Place mushrooms on paper towel, bottom side down to drain (about 15 minutes.)

In large mixing bowl add Crabmeat, egg, onions

Melt margarine mix with bread crumbs, put in mixing bowl.

Add mayonnaise and stir mixture well. (Should be the consistency of corn bread, a little on the stiff side, yet not like cake batter.)

Spray baking dish with Pam.

Stuff mushrooms with stuffing, place in oven an bake for about 15 minutes, or until they just start to brown.

Note: This recipe can be used to make stuffing for all sort of meats, chicken, chops, fish, and shrimp just to name a few.

SOURCE INFORMATION

AND

BIBLIOGRAPHY

ARTICLES, BOOKS, CALENDARS, MAGAZINES, AND MISC.

Allen Chapel Mens' Day Committee. Westside Church and Community Calendar. New Smyrna Beach: 1998.

Byrne, June. <u>Handbook for Genealogical Research in Central Florida</u>. Daytona. Daytona Beach Family History Center, 1999.

Daytona Beach News-Journal, New Smyrna Centennial Celebration (1987.)

Daytona Beach News-Journal, Volusia Magazine: Special Edition. (2006.)

Hawks, Dr. John Milton. Family Register. Edgewater: 1820s-1890s.

Hubbard, Royal. *Ancient and Modern New Smyrna and Vicinity, (*Gary Luther *annotated* 1997) (1906.)

Polk City Directories. <u>New Smyrna Directories</u>. 1950, 1954,1957, 1960, 1965, 1970, and 1975.

Sweet, Zella Wilson. *New Smyrna Beach and Neighboring Communities* (Ianthe Bond Hebel ed.,1998.)

INTERVIEWS

Personal and telephone interviews with individuals, business owners (past and present) family members, and friends in New Smyrna Beach, FL, (January through December 2006.)

MAPS

Sanborn Perris Map Company. *Fire Insurance Maps of New Smyrna and Coronado Beach, Volusia County, Florida*. New York, 1895, 1901, 1906, 1912, 1916, 1924, 1930.

REPOSITORIES

Black Heritage Museum, Inc., 314 North Duss Street, New Smyrna Beach, FL 32168.

City of Edgewater Leisure Service Department, 1108 South Ridgewood Avenue, Edgewater, FL 32132.

City of New Smyrna Beach, 210 Sams Avenue, New Smyrna Beach, FL 32168.

County of Volusia Clerk of Courts, 101 N. Alabama Avenue, Deland, FL. 32720.

County of Volusia Property Appraiser Office, 123 W. Indiana Avenue, Deland, FL. 32720.

Florida Bureau of Land Management, Eastern States, 7450 Boston Boulevard, Springfield, VA 22153-3121.

Florida Department of State, State Library and Archives of Florida; R.A. Gray Building, 500 South Bronough Street, Tallahassee, FL 32399, <http://www.floridamemory.com/Photographic Collection>.

Florida State Census. 1885, County of Volusia Library, City Island Library, Daytona Beach, FL 32114.

Historic Preservation Commission, 210 Sams Avenue, New Smyrna Beach, FL 32168.

New Smyrna Museum of History, 120 Sams Avenue, New Smyrna Beach, FL 32168.

University of South Florida (USF), Electronic Collections Department, 4202 E. Fowler Avenue, Tampa, FL 33620,< http://etc.usf.edu>.

University of South Florida (USF), Special Collections Department, 4202 E. Fowler Avenue, Tampa, FL 33620.

COUNTY, STATE, AND FEDERAL DOCUMENTS

Department of Commerce Bureau of Census. Fifteenth Census. 1930. Population. Volusia County. Washington, 1930.

_____. Fourteenth Census. 1920. Population. Volusia County. 1920.

_____. Thirteenth Census. 1910. Population. Volusia County. 1910.

_____. Twelfth Census. 1900. Population. Volusia County. 1900.

_____. Eleventh Census. 1880. Population. Volusia County. 1880.

_____. Tenth Census. 1870. Population. Volusia County. 1870.

_____. Ninth Census. 1860. Population Volusia County. 1860.

_____. Eighth Census. 1850. Population. Volusia County. 1850.

Bureau of Census. 1860. Slave Schedules. Volusia County. Washington, 1860.

_____. 1850. Slave Schedules. Volusia County. 1850.

Florida State Census. 1885. Population. Volusia County. Tallahassee. 1885.

INDEX

ABC

DEF

Everett, Clareese, 32
Fish, Shrimp, and Crab Industries, 12
Florida East Coast Railroad (FEC), 15
Floyd, Bee, 38 Floyd, Frank, 38
Forgotten Christmas Tree, 73
Franklin, George Manuel, 19, 62, 63, 117
Franklin, Jinnie Meeks, 117
Frazier, Herman, 36
Freeman, Pete, 37
Freeman, Morgan, 38
Freeman, Myrna, 38
Fullington, Darryl, 30

GHI

Gainous, Dr. Rabie, 24, 120
Gainous-Wynn Funeral Home, 120
Gaskin, Gregory, 107
Gaskin, Patricia Plummer, 107
General Foods, 99
Gilbolt, Mr., 25
Graham, Sammie, 88
Green Leaf Restaurant, 51
Green Machine Tree Service, 119
Green, Willie Mae, 68
Guinn, Effie, 78
Guinn, Walter, 78
 Harris, Darcia Warthaw, 85
Harris, Derrick, 85
Harris, Mr., (Boss Man), 39
Henderson, Hattie, 26, 69
Henderson, Henry Harry, 26, 69
Higgs and Son, 56, 60
Higgs, Richard, 60

Higgs, Robert, 60
Hill, Al, 59
Hill, Ellis (Sweet), 19
Hill, George, 72
Hill, Phalease, 59
Hill, Willie Mae Meeks, 19
Hives, Eurcell (Jackie), 78
Hives, Jimmie Lee, 78
Holzendorft, Charlotte, 49
Horne, Lee Woulard, 52, 53, 65
Horne, Roosevelt, 48, 49,52, 53, 65
Hospital, 27
Howard Teemer Painting, 113
Hudson, Fannie Minson, 85, 95
Hudson, James Sr., 94, 95
Hudson Plastering Service, Inc., 95
Huff, Hattie, 72
Hughes, Mr., 41
Hunter, William "Cat", 30
Hutchins, Laura, 76
Hutchins, Richard Sr., 76
Inner-City Enterprises, 100

JKL

J. Brendel Enterprises, Inc., 97
Jackson, James "JY", 40
Jackson, Louella Isaac, 40
Jackson, Marion, 66, 67
Jackson, Mary, 34
JC's Restaurant, 25
Jenkins and Son, 71
Jessup's Pawn Shop, 48
Jones, Darrell, 104
Jones, Dwayne, 104

Jones, Earl Sr., 104
Jones, James, 64
Jones and Jones Landscaping, 104
Jones, Virginia, 55,64
Jordan, Carlus, 68, 70, 71, 82, 101
Jordan, Emma Lou, 64, 68, 82
Jordan, Leandrus, 63, 68, 82, 101
Jordan, Novella, 68
Karen's Restaurant, 25
Korean War, 6
Lane, Leroy, 72
Lewis, Liza, 56
Lil' Neal's BBQ, 102
Lil Pop's" Professional Auto Detailing, 71, 101
Lipsey, Leroy, 49
Lipsey, Ola Mae, 49
Logan, Annie, 87
Louis, Joe, 82
Love, Louis (Hambone), 51
Loveless, Howard, 33, 100
Lowery, Annie 31, 41, 105
Lowey Brown Apartments, 111
Lowery, John (J.W.), 31, 41, 71, 101, 105
Lowery Service Station and Garage, 41

MNO
Madonna House, 31
Mann, Freddie 48 Manual Labor, 17
Marshall, Harold, 44,45,50
Marshall, Josie, 44,45,49, 50
Marshall, Nellie Alderman, 45
Marshall, Preston, 45
Mathis, Charles, 43, 103

Nursing Home, 27
OK Barbershop, 19, 117
Orange Groves, 13

PQR
Palace Café, 19
Pearson, James, 78
Pearson, Marilyn, 78
Pettis Court, 73
Pettis Park, 73
Pettis, Lydia, 21, 73
Powell, Mary, 47
Prescott, Mary, 21,22
Rainge, Gwendolyn, 51
Rainge, Henry J., 79
Rainge, Ophelia, 79
Ratcliff, Catherine, 23
Redemptive Fathers, 31
Reno, 57
Reese, Willie (Barber Reese), 21
Richards, Nancy, 49
Robinson, Dan, 56
Robinson, Eddie, 65
Robinson, Ola Mae, 54, 65
Rogers, Arzy, 88
Rogers, Clarence, 88
Rogers, Gordon Sr., 56, 88
Rogers, Louise, 20, 38
Robinson, Dan, 56
Robinson, Thelma, 56
Rollins, Mary, 77
Rollins, William, 77
Roosevelt's Playhouse, 53

STU

Saint Paul M.E. Church, 5, 20
Saw Mill, 14
Settle, Willis, 24, 120
Singletary, Cassandra, 77
Skin House, 46
Smith, Charles, 88
Smith, Henry, 58, 63
Smith, Mildred, 24, 120
Smith, Myrtis Davis, 51
Smith, Rosa, 58, 62
Snooks Place, 58
Stanley, Jasper, 55
Stanley, Nina, 55, 64
Star-Lite Beer Garden, 58
Star Theater, 52
Society's Place, 63
Southern Instruments, 77
Southern Oaks, 109, 110
Stubbs, Anna, 31
Stubbs, John, 31
Smyrna Funeral Home, 24, 120
Spot, The, 61
Spot Restaurant and Tourist Home, 56, 63
Tamishco, Inc., 103
Teemer, Edna 113
Teemer, Howard, 113
Thomas, Annie, 61
Thomas, Eugene, 61, 62
Thomas, Johnny, 61
Thompson, Cora, 57
Thompson, David, 57
Thompson, Estella, 58
Thompson, Robert (R.C.), 26

Thompson's Rooming, 46, 57
Thompson, Rudolph, 58
Thompson, Pearlie Mae Morris, 26
Turpentine Industries, 16
United States Armed Forces, 113
University of Florida (UF), 35

VWX

Vern Brown Automotive Repair Shop, 98
Vietnam War Veteran, 6, 99
Volusia County Health Department, 56
Volusia County Public Schools, 112
Wadley, Helen, 62
Wadley, Rufus (Uncle Rufus), 62
Wadley, Vicki, 23, 86
Walgreen Drug Store, 75
 Walker, Harry, 27
Walker, Lillie, 27
Walker, Wanda, 85
Wallace, Clara, 20
Wallace, James, 20
Waters Funeral Home, 116
Waters, Jennifer, 115, 116
Waters, Johnny, 35
Waters, Lavell, 116
Waters, Mattie, 35
Watson, John 20
Watson, Mina, 20
White, Antoinette, 118
White, Calvin "Bear", 118
Whitehead, Edith, 79, 88
Whitehead, Mallie, 79, 88
WIC Store, 85
Williams, Arthur "Art", 108

Williams, Arthur "Big John", 108
Williams, Clifford "Big Cliff", 23
Williams, Michael, 23, 99
Williams, Russelle, 108
Williams Tree Service, 108
Willie Woods Masonry, 98
Wilson, Rosa, 75
Wilson, Zeke, 75
Windom, John, 72
Woodard, James, 72
Woodard, Marie Walden, 72
Woods, Harriet, 98
Woods, Willie, 98
Wooten, Curtis, 56
Wooten, John, 42, 105, 106
WWI, 6
WWII, 6
WWII Veteran, 109
Wynn, Alexander III, 24, 120

YZ

Zow, Katherine, 86, 115, 116
Zow, Sam, 86, 115, 116
Zow Security Services, 86, 116

146

www.ingramcontent.com/pod-product-compliance
Lightning Source LLC
Chambersburg PA
CBHW052343090426
42740CB00039B/2185